Stars in Our Hearts

Tokens

Suzanne Hilary

EDITOR

World Poetry Movement

Utah

Stars in Our Hearts: Tokens

Library of Congress
Cataloging in Publication Data

ISBN 978-1-61936-041-9

Printed and manufactured in the United States of America by

World Poetry Movement
Utah

Foreword

I would like to take this opportunity to welcome all of our newly-published poets to the World Poetry Movement. By sharing your work with a larger audience, you have joined us in our pursuit to keep the art of poetry alive and thriving today. At WPM, we work with great purpose and genuinely believe anyone can achieve poetic success with the right amount of determination. Walt Whitman once said, "To have great poets, there must be great audiences," and our goal is to continue feeding and building today's poetry community. Right now, our nation is full of both budding and seasoned artists whose poetry has received national recognition, which also means that writers must also be readers in order for such recognition to be possible. By showcasing the work of aspiring writers and putting it out there for all to see, we hope to keep more readers and writers of all levels engaged to this artform. Any accomplished writer will agree that to become a better writer it is essential to also be an audience by reading the works of others just as often as one writes. To fellow aspiring poets, each individual poem in this collection shares a unique source of inspiration, offers a new idea or perspective, and/or displays a creative way to express sentiment and emotion. We hope you find just as much pleasure in reading the verse throughout as you do in composing your own. In the meantime, keep writing, keep sharing, and keep those dreams close to your heart!

Suzanne Hilary
Editor

Easter Bunnies See Their Shadows Too

I like to write in cursive.
It's harder to read and takes twice as long to write,
but the way the letters seductively fall into one another intrigues me.
My mother's in the kitchen making deviled eggs
and watching *Groundhog Day* on the little TV.
I can hear her mind contemplating money
Over the potent smell of those hard-boiled eggs
and that awful movie that I've never seen.
And sometimes I print my words;
because if the intoxication of those distractions
can't hide our problems,
seducing my eyes with a pretty font
won't stop me from reading her mind either.

Kendra Clay

I am seventeen years old and from a small town in northern Colorado. I write because I believe it is the most pure form of expression. It amazes me that within the simple words used every day, the right combination can offer a wealth of self-discovery. Writing is where the heart and mind blend to create a tapestry of expression and meaning. My hope is that others will take hold of my words, my tapestry, and find themselves in it.

spoken

to speak and never be heard
you yell scream and try to be heard
but everything you do someone knows
how to kill your powerful voice
your quiet till god comes and says
my child, you can always talk to me
and never have to yell or scream
even if no one else is here to listen and understand you
take your time to get your voice back
no pressure
they say silence is the best
sometimes just sit back and listen
watch and review
and when you do speak you will be heard

Meg'n Washington

Your Loss

I remember that one day
All the words you did say
Pretending everything's okay
I have to just walk away.

But I must say before I go
That I love you so
And every time you hold me near
I see everything crystal clear
When you look into my eyes
I look so hard to see your lies.

That's when you changed your mind
And the turn out wasn't kind,
You picked the one that lied
But thought I'd be on your side.

When you look back
And realize you're not intact
You'll remember me
And will want me to be
Forever and always on your side
But instead you picked the one that lied.

Alexa Brady

Not Afraid to Love

I'm not afraid to love,
I never have been.
I'm not afraid to give,
I've always had the urge.
I no longer feel the pain of others not
wanting to love me,
all I can do is love them in return.
I no longer feel the hurt and guilt
from my past,
because I'm learning to let go...
even thought it's not easy...
(The hardest battle I've ever endured),
but I know something great is waiting for me
as soon as I win.
I'm not afraid to love,
I'm not afraid to give,
to cherish,
to keep,
or to hold,
I'm not afraid to embrace.
I'm no longer scared to open my heart,
I'm no longer scared to show my scars,
I'm no longer afraid to say
"Yes I've been hurt,
yes I was abused,
mistreated,
sexually harassed,
and taken advantage of.
Yes I was bullied,
and broken,
and my soul had died..."
But I gained my strength,
began to love myself,

and love you too...
even if you don't feel the same...

Sarah Christmas

I wrote this poem after I finally had an epiphany about life and the issues I was going through. This poem is my break-through and the beginning of a magnanimous journey we all call life. Poetry is everything I stand for.

If I Were Free

If I had one day to be free,
I would spend that day to be me.
No one to tell me what to say
or how to dress or when I can't play,
I would stay inside and sit in the dark,
and listen to music, then sing like a lark.
I would sit and think about all I can do,
like go into town or dye my hair blue.
I could jump around, be live and giddy
or lay on the couch like a lazy old kitty.
Oh, I wish I were free one day, just for me.
But that cannot be because I'm not free.

Harmony Angel Bade

The Day She Left

A moment of silence like two strangers who just met
with an awkwardness feeling like love never did exist,
Goodbye to something that could have been or something that never
    was?
Confused is all I got out of her as she walks away into the dark
without a backwards glance.
I stand there alone as usual and wonder why was I handed another
    chance?
She torments me again by turning around and coming back with one
    last embrace
just to be torn apart as she turns to leave my place.
I have had enough of the broken hearts
because it hurts too much when they so easily tear it apart.
Love only exists to make you realize how cold the human race can
mimic something so pure, so innocent,
but to me is slowly becoming non-existent.
It is hard not to have feelings of hatred toward someone that you
    thought was so beautiful and loving,
but turned out to be so cold and uncaring.
You try not to feel used, but no matter what you do,
your heart reminds you of the chance that you took for that long-
    lasting embrace.
I dare not try to tell her that I still love her
because that would be like adding fuel to the fire, hoping that the flame
    would last.
She is gone now and I can feel the emptiness surrounding me like I'm
    its prey.
I believe I was meant to be alone and to never find the one who would
    never let go.

Patricia Sandoval

Can You See Me?

Can you see me? I am the past that people don't want to see
I am the past that others refuse to believe
Can you see me? I am the future
The future that brings pity, shame and fear to those who wish not to
    see it
Can you see me?
Can you see how the blind have sight?
Can you see how the seeing are blind?
Can you see me? I am the present that people throw around and pay
    no attention to
I am the present that longs to be understood and accepted
Can you see me? I am what some people call a figure of your
    imagination
Can you see me? I have been around since the beginning of time
I will be here for eternity
Can you see me?
Do you even know what I look like?
Do you know who I am?
Allow me to reintroduce myself
My name is Truth

Nia Anderson

My World

My world is like a library,
Books piled on top of each other.
Every time it gets too heavy my library breaks and falls.
But you should know better than to worry,
Because I build it up again.
My world is full.
My world is steady.

Iemawn Chughtai

Welcome Back

We missed you while you were away,
But indeed, we thought about you every day.
We are so delighted to have you back,
And that's just a true and simple fact.

We missed you like an ocean without waves,
Like a flower without rain,
Like a musician without an instrument,
Like a poet without words.

We counted the days, the hours, the minutes,
And even the seconds until your return.
That day has finally arrived and your family welcomes you home again.
We welcome you with open arms,
Renewing bonds of love that we had formed.

Welcome back!
We surely missed you a lot.
Welcome back!
It's good to have you in your favorite spot.

Gracie C. Davis

The Prime Hound

I wait
For her existence to disintegrate
Into pure love…
For her reach to no longer touch the boundaries
Of comfort.
I am not organized to feel
The expressive struggle
Of internal disappointment,
Her eyes a cavernous haze of memories,
Her smile sizeable, but opaque to the earth.
She is timeworn,
And I, the adolescent, suffer the decay of another.
Questions fill me with false self-control.
Hound and child flourish, but the interval will emanate
And I will not be willing
To lose an irreplaceable friend.

Alex Staub

My Angel

Your sparkling blue eyes and soft silky skin
held close and peaceful to my breasts.
The infant that just a few minutes before
was cradled so warm in my womb and at rest.

My cherished infant daughter was finally here,
more innocent than anything I'd ever known.
From that single moment on, my heart was yours,
my unending love for you was then etched in stone.

As I lovingly held you next to my heart my dear
days turned to months, as you did gracefully grow.
Then one special day that first step you did take,
independence, curiosity and amazement did flow.

Throughout your young life, my presence close by
from dawn until dusk we strived to survive,
but sometimes my decisions would cause you to cry.
Moments in time, I failed but lovingly always tried.

Some choices then did not always reflect
the caring and nurturing you so much deserved.
During night's darkness, your fear, quiet and somber,
was your deepest secret as I much later learned.

Still you looked up with that childish smiling face.
It would never compare to the star's twinkling rays.
Onward we marched forward, a bright new day to share
bringing with us strength which would truly amaze.

You are now a stunning woman and thoughtful mom
with babes of your own, each one so secure
in the knowledge that whatever their lives may bring,
hardship, fear and want they will not endure.

Each one is cherished dearly with the passing years.
Your spirit, I pray, finally rests happily inside.
For your family needs you to nourish and to teach
many lessons, you'll do well; take life in stride.

Always when I am with you, my love for you grows
and my spirit overflows with pride and amazement.
It is quieted now as I marvelously watch you mature
facing challenges; the Lord's grace to you is sent.

I ponder; God lent you to me to love and to guide.
He trusted my judgement and courage, always to care.
My tender, beloved, sweet, sensitive daughter…
My everlasting rewarding privilege to bear.

Brenda Fisher

Lovers' Poems

Master	Slave
she is skin	he is milk
tasted	honeyed
caressed	sweet and clingy
rich bitter	like syrup oozing
like coffee	from maple
she is my beauty	he is stuck on me
the sun rising	he is the sky turned
and setting luxuriously	pinky orange
colored	before my ascent
my midnight	the purple curtains
siren singing softly	closing
in silky moonlight	behind me
only	
I am hers	the moon pulling my tides
	the starlight dazzling
	in my eyes
	he is wholly mine
	I his

Brionne Janae

Love Will Be Here

Love will be here
You hold my heart in your hands, I've seen you smile,
I've seen you in pain and loneliness,
waiting for someone to love you the way you were meant.
Years have passed since you

Jeremy Larson

My Thought Is Abstracted

Where is this wavelength
a common place of frequency?
My heart's isolated
where is my society?
I am not better
but where is everyone?
These differences of opinion
make my head ache
My thought is abstracted
where do these memories come from?
Lost and found is my soul
these scars of somewhere else
Can't let go of what I don't have
Reunite, reunite
buried are these connections
where are the pieces?
My eyes are fading
My ears are crying
for familiar voices of days gone by
My lucky horseshoe
was thrown in the river
Truth it hurts
but my song it is painful
Am I not ready?
Do they not want me?
My reality's drifting
ground under me shifting
This world I've outgrown
can't survive here alone
My onlookers tear up
and my face it is dripping
Blank stares, I escape
while my mind it is slipping

Jennifer Cline

The Cost of Causes

Skeptics running left and right
Heroes flying out of sight
Greedy speedy money-makers
Empty shallow money wasters

Poisonous politics taking place
Our world must feel what's on her face
Causes causing public fee
Laced with such hypocrisy

Global Warming! We need change
So name the changes that you've made?
We all know what we want to see
What should change and what should be

Evil corporations, that's all they are
You hate oil but drive a car?
Recycle paper! That's what you wrote
On fifteen hundred sticky notes

Capital commerce, business best
Scandals, treason, all the rest
Pushing, prodding, preaching too
They all will tell us what to do

What to say and how to say it
Depends on who appreciates it
Green is good but selling's sad
Fair trade is cool! But oil's bad.

Radical, righteous, good and free
Fighting's evil can't you see?
War is bad that's no debate
But who controls unlicensed hate?

Bush is stupid, Cheney too?
How can you say what they should do?
Think your own thoughts and keep your beliefs
But check yourself before you speak

It's not the cause that takes the toll
But In the way we play our role
Forceful claims, breeding hate
Zero research, no debate

It may seem good to give out rice
Save the poor, set coffee's price
Do farmers save on these resources?
Or do their buyers sign divorces

Next time you quote the Constitution
First look around for the solution
Through the woodwork, behind the door
Outside or Orwell's *Eighty-Four*...

Joel Gerhardt

Last Day of Camp

As the camp day began
the last day came to an end

The journey of the woods
has been so good
I wish it wouldn't end
the way it should

It's sad that time has gone
I've grew a bond with everyone

It's been a wonderful time
with laughter and tears
It's hard to say goodbye after all these years

Though we depart from the circle
your faces will always be engraved in my heart

Sharona Taylor

Just a Thought

Why does she keep thinking that he belongs to her?
She had faced her "ugly truth" already,
but somehow her heart refuses to face it.
She's dying, we're losing her.
She isn't the same anymore, because of him she changed somehow.
She tries every day to forget him, but there it comes,
the fact that she always wanted to know about him,
to know if they have at least something in common,
like their favorite baseball team, the New York Yankees,
or like they both like Switchfoot,
all those little details about him caught her completely.
She's so stoked on him, she's dying to find him somewhere
to say at least "Hi" to him, but unfortunately their fate doesn't want
    that,
maybe they aren't meant to be as she thought.

Even if they have everything in common, it doesn't mean they have
    to know it,
at least he doesn't have to.
She loves him, even if she denies it.
She wants to change that before it's too late.
She's trying, but it is not that easy to forget somebody like him;
he's the personification of her dream boy that's for sure.

He's totally happy right now, he's doing what he loves.
Even though she isn't the one who gives him the happiness,
she feels happy for him, he's making his dreams true.

It's just a thought, nobody has to know.

Yamel Tolentino

If Winter Comes

Winter sits
in quiet meditation
upon her cushion
Earth

White-mantled
her encrystalled breathing
rising on the crackling air

Mask-like
her face a cold, hushed, calm
Pensive with not-knowing

Waiting, gravid
with blood red tulips, bright streams
and a thousand, thousand larks

Fully present
to the coming birth of spring
and her own sweet dying

Jeannie O'Craighan

dark dream

i saw her with a man of such
my jealousy take the best side of me
with no reason to think of how
i go in my way to misery

i leave you this letter
to tell you i find my way back home
i'm sorry for hurting you but i must
my love once shined for you
this time it turned off

i was thinking how i left her
with my family in two hands
she's the greatest she just doesn't know it
my love never turned off for her

screaming how much i love her
she holds the knife that will put an end to life
my soul told her what mistake was in a dream
it's willing to die for her any second of any moment

does she know?
does she know how special
she is?

Garry Francois

Tell Me Something, Baby

Tell me something, baby,
Do you love me like I love you?
I don't know why I'm asking,
Because I already know you do.
It started with a hello,
Continued with a hi,
But if there's one thing I can't do,
It's telling you goodbye.
Tell me something, baby,
Do you promise that you'll try,
When all else is crazy,
To never say goodbye?
I promise to try too,
To try harder at finding joy,
Because one thing I shall never do
Is play you like a toy.
Tell me something, baby,
Is the picture of us the same?
Has it changed drastically,
Or does it bear the same name?
Do you still believe that growing older,
I'll be by your side?
Or do you think as the days grow colder
To me you can't confide?
Let me tell you something, baby.
You're all I'll ever want,
Because being with you is natural,
It's not some stupid stunt.
If you don't know yet,
Let me tell you now,
You have all of my heart,
More than I'd dare to allow.

Emily Townsend

The Studio Where I Belong

It's where I roam,
It's my part-time home,
The studio
Is where I belong.

It's what keeps me alive,
It's my everlasting strive,
And I'm sure you can see
I'm a dancer at heart.

The studio
Where I belong
Is a place you couldn't imagine.
When I walk in the doors I stop and think,
"Finally—home sweet home."

The studio
Where I belong
Is a place I'd rather be.
It's the only place that I can be
Where I can just dance freely.

Now you see
What's important to me.
My only wish would be
That you would just agree.
The studio
Is where I belong.

Amanda Keaty

hey stranger

hey stranger,
i love you.
you'll never know,
but i love you.
hey stranger,
you'll never know
just how much
i really care,
just how much
i treasure you,
all of you,
and how much
i want you,
all of you,
good or bad,
i don't care,
all of you.
but i'll never be
what i need to be
in order to be
all that you'll ever need.
hey stranger,
i love you.
you'll never know,
but I love you.

Mary Lucille Sawyer

Sleep

The comforting breeze
laughing softly though the window
blows across my face.
Fresh air swirls my hair
in curls across my pillow.
The moonlight shines
in my eyes,
as I stare
into the face of the celestial body above me.
My head is filled with thoughts
of the day and the one to come,
of the future and past,
of him and her,
of this and that.
I close my tired eyes and start
to dream
of lands far away.
Of adventures and romance.
At heart I'm still a child
who dreams of freedom
far from rules and expectations
far from drama and disputes.
I wait every moment
of every never-ending day
for my sweet retreat
to a land of fairy tales and lost wishes.
I wait and wait
for peace to lend an escape.
I wait and wait
for sleep to find me.

Amber Miller

His Note

One day he walked in and there she was,
The most beautiful girl he ever saw.
Every day, at the same time,
And at the same table he admired her.

A mere waitress, she walks over and smiles,
He stares and orders.
Every day, at the same time,
And at the same table,
He ordered the same thing.

And every day, she knew he would arrive,
At the same time, sit at the same table,
And order the same thing.

A rainy day came and he was there,
Though something was different.

He got up, she watched him leave,
This day, at that time,
From that table.

When she went to the table,
There was a note, she read the note,
She gazed up and stared at the rain.

That day, at that time,
From that table, his note said,
"I love you."

Emely Ventura

Metamorphosis

Remember that girl?
That girl that used to be bubbly, wild, free
And is now the bitch you rage about to no one because
She stole your boyfriend, or spilled wine on your favourite blouse,
Or called you names behind your back, or—
You actually can't remember why you hate her.
But, every time you see her, you see red
And maybe that red is spilt blood.

Now, this realization comes much later
Perhaps in the last moments spent lying on your death bed
Where you wish you could go back and change everything, anything,
    something
So that maybe you wouldn't be lying there, dying right then
(You hated her so much, it killed you).
Once a mere seed planted innocently into fertile ground, it has
Infected your whole world
Torn your true blue sky into shreds that rain black.
You grew your whole life around that monolith you just couldn't let go
    of
And it pulled you right down to your underwater tomb
Where you stayed.

Remember that girl?
That girl that used to be bubbly, wild, free?
You used to be her.

Xiu Qi Chin

If Anyone Asks

It's just another night with a giant broken heart
Misery around me, days I don't know how to start
In a room shaded in black like a cloud of loneliness
Half a bottle of wine is all the pride I've got left
If anyone asks you better tell a lie
'Cause I don't want him to know
That I was ever here, sulking on the floor
Soaking up pain, tears that fly galore
Half a bottle of breakup wine
Because if you knew, don't think I'd ever stop crying
Don't say that I was here wishing I was dying
I'm soaking in fire, getting burned to the bone
Lot's of pain and suffering and I'm all alone
In a cold place of memories, pictures, letters and pain
Trying to keep myself together, wish this life I contained
If anyone asks you better tell a lie
'Cause I don't want you to know

Cassandra Potratz

My name is Cassie Potratz. I've been a writer since I was a young child. I'm actually a musician and my poem is actually a song I wrote when I was twelve. Now I'd like to dedicate this song to my ex-boyfriend C.R.S.

The Light

In the darkness of the night,
I closed my eyes to see the light.
Your words are cruel,
My pain is real,
I cannot describe the way I feel.
With every lie that you told,
It was your heart that grew more cold.
I am stronger now,
My future bright.
I closed my eyes and saw the light.

Amy Kerns

Comfort

As I look into your eyes
All fear dies
As I lie in your arms
All harm done seems like none
As I listen to your heart
I feel as if we could never be apart
As I kiss your soft lips
I can't help but wish you were all that exists
As I freak and think of what could go wrong
You use that perfect voice
And simply say it will all be okay
Despite all reasoning
All facts
That one act
Sends me falling even deeper than before
Wanting nothing more than to ignore
My mind's post wars
But only because I can't help but want you for forevermore

Cassandra Lein

Every Time

Every time you think of me,
I hope you get a migraine.
Every time you wonder about why I don't call you anymore,
I hope you get lost in your thoughts.
Every time tears fall from your eyes,
I hope it's not because of me.
Every time you say my name in vain,
I hope you realize the pain you brought upon my heart.
Every time you want to break down and text me,
I hope your phone dies.
Every time you go to drive by my house,
I hope your car doesn't start.
Every time you hear our song,
I hope the station goes out.
And most of all,
when you start to realize I was right,
I hope you are alone.

Chrissy Sell

Sk8er Boi's Love Song

Several tears, several fears but never too much.
I'm with you every step of the way,
like you say I make you smile.
But what the hell, right?
I mean Alice has fallen down some holes, and so have we, but no matter
    what,
we'll have a happy ending.
I know I'm a sk8ter boi,
but you're my girlfriend and I love you.
When you're gone I wish you were here.
So just know you're always in my heart and I never let go of you.

Allyssa Bollmann

My Daughter

I remember cradling you in my arms
When you were a precious little baby.
I know I tried to keep you from harm
Looking toward your future joys and sorrows.

You slowly grew into a beautiful girl
That couldn't wait to run and play.
Sometimes all I could be was proud
Even in times when there was nothing I could say.

The more you grew up and learned
The closer we started to become.
I am so happy to have the bond we do
Because it helps me to see everything anew.

The bond has made us best friends,
Friendship to exist without end.
When you are away, I miss you.
You never go too far away but it's still hard.
I'm so proud to have you as my daughter,
All because of the fact that I love you.

Melynda Daugherty

A Lament for the Wicked

A crimson rose
Beauty beholding
Petals free falling
slowly unfolding

Bleeding out ink
Carved elegant prose
Etched into skin
A name unknown

A woeful existence
Extinguished flame
Mercurial heartbeat
A courageous lamb

Follow the footsteps
A deplorable essence
Desperate for love
but knowing inadequacy

Erynn Billue

Take the Reins

What happened to this generation?
I thought that we were the inspiration
that would ensure that your perspiration
would be spent on saving the world
and saving the system that makes us all free.
I thought that our actions would be
remembered as cosmic determination
since we laid out our dreams like a flag unfurled.

What happened to this generation?
Your heads down to your phones, heads down to the drone
of a futureless future.
You care less about others, more about self
You've sold out to the man, you're a slave on his shelf.
Not thinking, not acting, not feeling the cure
You know you could be to this planet's disease,
It's too hard to reach out or get down on your knees.

What happened to this generation?
We wanted peace, love, no war.
We looked out to the stars and felt the earth's core.
You look out on a lot filled with cars, but empty stores.
They fill the cities because people can't work.
The jobs, they are missing, the money's run out.
You could do something about it, you have the clout
but you don't and you won't and it's all about doubt.

What happened to this generation?
Is there hope that you'll rise and open your eyes,
and take the reins from the driver who drives despair into the
veins of the helpless, the homeless, the unhappy,

this unfair hapless reckoning from those who don't share.
It's time you make meaning, and leave a legacy behind.
That you took a stand, you were just and were kind.
And you took away the power, you, no longer blind,
from the ones on Earth's playground
who never played fair.

Darrah Welfare

Nightmare

Jerked awake from disturbing dreams,
Terror fills my invoiced screams,
Another night of restless sleep
with sweat-soaked covers all aheap.

Breathe deep to calm my racing heart.
Await the dawning day to start,
Another day of fear and fright
of what dreams may come tonight.

Will they be dreams sharp and pointed
or images so disjointed?
Dreams in colors of violet-dread
with flames and sparks of yellow-red.

Or scenes of love turned to hate,
disappointments that don't abate,
Worse—the loneliness dark as coal
that eats away your very soul.

The nightly tide of ebb and flow,
The dreams retreat but do not go.
They have always returned to me.
There is nowhere that I can flee.

Some nights the dreams, they do not haunt,
they do not scare, they do not taunt,
but just hide away in the dark
and bide their time to make their mark.

I pray this night I shall have peace,
One night's rest, one night's release.
A night without a dream's visit,
It's not too great a prayer—is it?

Rick Christopher

School Days

S-school is a place to teach and learn
C-context that influences the meaning of words that are taught
H-handbook with information about difference subjects
O-outstanding student in the classroom
O-overlooked question on the MSPAP
L-literacy and ability to read and write in our modern world

D-definition that explained as one
A-alphabets that we use to write proper language
Y-years we attend school for 180 days
S-salute our American every day

Tanora Gough

Always

I remember your eyes, sky blue,
As my heart breaks with feelings so true.
All your words scream in my head,
while my body twists and turns in bed.

The echoes of silence fill the room,
The rose of regret is in full bloom.
I should of hugged you goodbye,
Who knew we had run out of time?

Morning will come, you'll still be missed,
Lips trembling from when we last kissed.
I'll walk the day, I'll play the part,
Without my soul for you'll always have my heart.

Jessica Hayden

Trying Not to Disappear

I am trying not to disappear
in a world that, in a time, moves so fast.
The world is at war in the streets and at home.
I have to hold on tight and be strong
New ways to consume me are being developed
They know where my weakness is.
They aim there.
I have to be strong not to disappear
To be there when the morning comes and last out
the storm.
When will it end?
I hope not when I disappear!

Debra Cox

Bubbles of Blessings

Bubbles of blessings fill my bathtub
as I soak on Friday night
although I ponder all the world events
and the awful daily plight
We all struggle to get by these days
Sometimes I feel so sad
With politics and the economy
it seems our country has gone mad
Each day I do the best I can
and wish I could do more
As time goes by I'm longing
to be home on Heaven's shore
But I know God has a plan for me
That's why He's left me here
perhaps to guide some other soul
beyond the growing fear
So I'll focus on the good things
that I enjoy each day
and remember all the blessings
that God has brought my way
I will soak away the tension
and relax away the stress
I will pray to God, our Savior
that we'll pass this grueling test
I'll be content right where I am
and seek God's guiding light
I'll count my many blessings
in the bathtub every night

Wendy Garvey

Pieces to the Puzzle

A picture's worth a thousand words but a puzzle is worth more.
The smooth pieces and cookie cutters that lay scattered on the kitchen
floor
Are threads of beads and words alike in every person's tale.
Each piece placed side by side will set a special ship to sail.
A puzzle is more than pieces;
A puzzle is more than games.
Each and every puzzle piece will shift through great measures, words
and names.
Lurking in the shadows or boldly placed in the center,
Once pieces are set they can't be moved and time can't be reentered.
On odd occasions pieces are lost in the murkiness of doubt and despair.
And some may never be retrieved,
Of this you must beware.
But pieces painted black are numbered very few.
Each piece of vital light was made by love for you.
So look upon your many pieces of pure hope undefeated,
And hope, one day, your puzzle will be completed.

Madison Sweitzer

Love

Love ruled my heart
    and life throughout!
It flourished my imagination
    with cute coloration!
It took me to the land
    of evergreen beauty!
It showered me with
    unceasing flow of smiles!
It mesmerized my moments
    with powerful impacts!
It took me to the height
    of true, deep happiness!
It embraced my lovely soul
    with lasting liveliness!
It created series of laughter
    echoing loud joys forever!
It granted me blessings of life
    among hard, harsh realities.

Tarlika Desai

I Am a Stranger

I am a stranger, but you are not to me...
We have known each other all through eternity
You have been sitting beside me on my journey in life
We have traveled far together, over land and sea
We have sung and danced together, you and me
I have looked in your eyes and have seen my sorrow
Your tears were my tears, as we brushed them aside
You have laughed with me when life was brighter
As you are playing your guitar, I am the strings you're feeling
As you are singing, I am the voice you're hearing
So long for now, my special friend forever
I am a stranger, but you are not to me.

Sandra Discetta

Lake Water

Early in the morning, the water appears to look like a mirror
No movement, ripples, waves, just still
As the breeze begins and movement starts
You begin to hear water moving towards the shore

Water rushing the shore, splashing on the rocks
Wave after wave smoothly one after another
Smooth sounds, quiet and serene
Water moves on and following the current

A slight ripple appears in the mirror-looking water
Up pops a loon riding low in the water
Slowly moves along, hardly making a ripple
A blink of your eye and it is gone

Florence Brick

A Young Man's Dream

Once to me, a story was told,
Of a young man, brave and bold,
Who crossed over the mountainside
Across the great valley wide

In search of his life's dream.
Though he searched, it did not seem
His dream would ever come in sight,
Though he searched with all his might.

He looked for it in the babbling brook,
Longed for it in each chance he took.
Job after job, town after town,
Still, his dream could not be found.

On his journey, he happened to meet
A girl so fair and oh so sweet.
"Through the course of time," said he,
"She shall become my bride to be."

Now they walk down the path of life,
Through the years as man and wife.
Now satisfied, the old man beams.
Could it be love was his dream?

Evelyn Bay

Neighborhood Flow

The sun is out.
The future is playing outside running after each other.
Their laughter fills in the silent corners, birds across the clear, blues skies.
Their mom's trying to get them to go inside because the sun is shining too bright that the mom's earrings are reflecting the light off them like disco balls.
Teens lying outside in the grass, attracting sun as if they were solar panels, eyes half way closed, tired, bored lazy is all that is left to be seen in their eyes.
Sound of chained basketball hoop annoying them, the screams of the different generations playing basketball, their sweat dripping like the tears of the girl who just got her heart broken.
"I wanna play" the 7 year old screamed. From a few feet away you can hear their response, laughter adds to the noise.
"Yo kid, get out of here. Can't you see were playing a game?" One of the guys yells at a kid who comes to the court and starts shooting a soccer ball. Hitting it off the wall, the sound adds on to the dribbling of the basketball.
The noise together may sound like a fully-operating orchestra, like Yo Yo Ma playing a solo.
To some being just a noise and to others the beat to their daily life, where they just spit out the flow and continue to grow.
As the sun drops, drops the basketball to the floor, the tired bodies to bed, and the confidence of the kid who couldn't play. They all disappear.
The place that held the beat to their daily life is silent.
Silence has now gathered.
Moonlight shining on the shoe a kid left behind, the basketball hoop that at one point in the day brought noise,
but they'll be back tomorrow when the sun is out for another neighborhood flow.

Carlos De La Rosa

Lust Speaks Boldly

Sexual desires are what makes me known;
and I will teach you things before you have grown.
Never worry about the ones who play hard-to-get
because I have lies and deception that have withstood all tests.
My work is endless without consideration of anyone's emotions;
but seeking to understand love and caring will hinder my thrilling
    motions.
Therefore, take heed to the physical feel-good and ignore trust;
and eventually you learn all the devious schemes through me, your
    devilish friend, Mr. Lust!

Anthony G. Gueory

Sleepless

Click clock,
Tick tock
Chants the monster on my wall.
Sleepless
I watch fingerless hands
Waving down at me.
Time drags with them,
Seconds, minutes, hours
Fold neatly into a blanket of time.
The monotonous chorus,
A tedious tune,
Miry mind teeters
On verge of insanity.

Counting sheep.
Legs...
Tails too.
Mind churning blurry thoughts
Of a thick bitter butter called life
Tossing and turning
Yearning for a peace
Constantly elusive.
See windows paling
Night softly slipping out!
Sleep embraces gently,
Then the alarm
Blurts obtrusive obscenities!
I had a dream....
There is no rest for the wicked!

Emily Masiane

Fallen Hero

A soldier fell today
A brave young man is dead
And for this fallen hero
Many tears are shed.

He served his country well,
Willingly with pride,
And he went to serve in battle
Knowing he might die.

He left the ones he loved
And off to war did go.
He fought for life and liberty
For people he didn't know.

He was true to his beliefs
Through sacrifice and pain.
He gave his life for others,
His service not in vain.

A soldier fell today.
A brave young man is dead.
And for this fallen hero
Many tears are shed.

Brenda Motley

Into the Light

I'm down under the dark
looking up into the light.
Wanting desperately to emerge
means with all of me, I must fight.
Knowing where I'm going
reveals my span of flight.
I'm down under the murk
reaching for the light.
Toiling through the earth
I begin to caress the air.
Breathing life above my shadow
I lure into the glare.
Submerged beneath the gloom
I await a vision of light.
Now standing above ground
I have ultimately seized my plight.
I'm no longer beneath the doom
it is now trapped beneath me.
I will never surrender to quandary
until no longer can I fight.
Which means I am now settled
up into the light.

Tori Kelly

God's Library

Our lives are like an open book that many hearts will read,
each year another chapter that reveals the life we lead.
When the book is finished, it's God that makes the test.
He will it go into His library, where He just selects the best.

Harold Gifford

The End of Everything

Insanity bleeds into her soul
Broken by scars of shame
Blackness fills her dreams.
The sickness screams.
Weakened by the thrill, she cries.
Memories fade away.
Existing life buried inside
A desecrated structure.
Trapped in a world of illusion.
She ignores the pain.
The innocence dissipates
As delicate creations ask why.
Reality cannot be faced.
Behind closed doors
Poison penetrates every last drop
Forgetting the devastating truth.
Numb to the never-ending pretending.
Reinforcing the oblivion
Trapped inside a home with empty bones
And the voices say:
    "Run away, baby, run away.
      Hide in a black hole.
      Tear apart your soul,
        Now you're out of control.
        Run away, baby, run away.
        Cold feet slide on through.
        Naked and afraid,
       This is true.
       Run away, baby,
       Run away,
      Baby,
      Run away."
                     Then everything ends.

Nicole MacDonald

illinois

many miles, miles to go, right before i rest again.
90 miles, miles from home, miles from heart, miles from friend,
miles from love, miles from fear, miles from start, miles from end.
you'll be there when I'm here. 7 days until then.

many days, days to go, until you make your final choice.
these next days will come and flow. with the sun will set the noise.
days to go, days to come. I made them cry, all those boys.
growing old and dreaming young, it is a city: illinois.

many meals, all to go, serving till the goal is met.
many seeds left to sow, memories i'll just forget.
help me keep my memory. every note adds more regret.
you will not remember me. but treasure now, this sunset.

Jaymyria Etienne

Untamed Love

I will love you no matter what,
Even if you have a baboon heart.
I will love you in a plane above the sky.
I will love you in the clouds on high.
I will love you more than marmalade on toast,
While taking a drive along the coast.
I will love you more than chocolate hearts
And we will never be apart.
I will love you until I die.
You are the apple of my eye.
You are the sunshine in my life.
I would love you as my wife.
Loving you is like ice cream
You are sweeter than my dream.
What makes my world go 'round?
My soul mate I have found.
To know you and to love you,
To need you and to see you,
You are like a dream come true.
I am so grateful I found you.
Loving you is like a carnival, for hours I would stand in line.
I will love you forever and ever. You are truly mine.

James Davis

Reunited

A clock on the wall
The second hand ticking and echoing in this quite room
Waiting in this room for the voice of an angel or that of a demon
Not knowing what is going to come through that door
Do I hide in fear or stay relaxed as an angel's hand guides me?
A voice faint but definitely a voice
Sweat starts to run down my face
The moment draws closer
What to expect, what to do
The door opens and in comes a man all smiles
He sits me down and asks about school
I feel relieved when he says this
His voice so smooth
Then he leans forward and says 5 words
These 5 words, life altering words
"I have some bad news"
My life thrown in to a blender
Then the news
The blender turned on, my life turns to chaos
Everything gets mixed
Up , down, left, and right no longer distinct
Nothing left to say
I cannot speak
I leave and go to my car.
The long drive home allows me to think
I am strong! I can get through this, I will not Fall!
I keep saying this to myself...home, finally home
I walk to my room my head spinning as I hit the mattress
Blackness...I wake hours later. It is late, my world still a mess.
I dig through the wreckage trying to find something to relate to,
trying to find an exit
A glimpse catches my eyes. I dig and wait. What is this?
Now an enemy but once a friend

A shimmering memory in this chaos
Stained with the marks of my past
But yet this small tool is the only thing in know in this now hell
Silence, we are alone. Do I open up for this old friend or walk away?
The words from the man repeat in my head
That's it. Hello friend, I say. I pause for a moment
What's one going to do? Only once, I press in, memory pour into me
I phase out, remembering all the times that this friend was there for me
Never judging, I am back. I look to my friend and see not 1, no not 2,
but 4
The familiar line
The puddle on the floor
A small stream along my arm
I have failed the test
I have lost
I am sorry

Dustin McGillivary

No BTR Without You!

There's no Big Time Rush without you,
What would Kendall do without a sister as pretty as you?
The show would rock but only halfway,
Without your smile to brighten the day.

Raffi Hernandez

Soul, Mind and Body (Just Breathe)

The world fluctuates the deeper you breathe
It flows towards the highest prestige
If you know you, then you know me
I can be anything, anything you want me to be
Follow the wind it will allow you to see
Just breathe
If you follow the river it will lead you to sea
and life will reveal itself as a great barrier reef
The water is pure and believe you me
that knowledge is found within every tree
You can be anything, anything you want to be
Follow your heart and don't allow others to lead
Just breathe
So raise your hands, let me see
those that know and practice how to be
The world is yours, your body is the machine
Explore your life path and don't be mean
So you can do anything, any dream possibly
and take it all in—it's for you and me
Just breathe

Thomas Bailes

How I Feel

Let me tell you how I feel,
Oh I can't believe how this just got real.
Such harsh words, definitely me and you it has killed.
See, I am confused but yet I understand.
I am sad but feeling happy, I've lost my heart, but I still have my soul,
which is warm but yet I still feel cold.
Let me tell you how I feel, see, I am not perfect and I have made
    mistakes,
unprepared and unrealistic, the important and key things in life,
man, I seemed to have missed it.
Oh how I wish I could kiss it!
It is too late
for my river is now polluted with fate.
Let me tell you how I feel
and now I know that how I feel is real.

Amanda Clayton

"How I Feel" symbolizes the constant obstacles I have encountered in my life. Through my poetry I hope to reach out to others who may be experiencing strife and struggle. Life is a struggle but it is grand also.

You'll Never Know

You'll never know, dear, how much I love you.
I want to spend every waking moment with you.
I want to spend the long nights of cold winters in your arms.
I want to spend hours in your arms under the stars during the warm
summer nights; I want to walk long distances with you, picking out
every color of the autumn leaves, and lie with you under covers during
the springtime rains.
I want to fall asleep listening to your every breath and wake up to the
steady beat of your heart.
For you will never know, dear, how much I love you.

Karlee Danner

Welcome

Welcome, welcome,
please come in.
Ascertain what it's like
to be me from within.
The door to my mind is always open
for most passages and rooms,
save a few I must keep hidden
from those who would abuse.
Hurry! If we hurry
we might just catch a glimpse
of what is few and far between
left of my innocence.
Ooh look! Way in the back
right next to guilt and shame,
you can see the light still burning
from a young man's lustful flame.
Now as we move along
I feel I must instruct
that you not linger too long
here in the foyer of bad luck.
Duck! Duck!
It was fast but did you spot it?
Be wary of euphoria,
my natural narcotic.
Now you may perceive it seems to be
the walls are closing in,
but it's only an illusion
cast by vacillating sins.
Chill? Oh, the chill you feel
is just a scanty frost.
Come back to haunt my inner thoughts
and cast by love long lost.
Forthwith we pass this portal,
if you peer in you'll see
the hope that perhaps someday
a better man I'll be.
Ahead there lies companionship
and devotion to my friends.

And I pray that they discern
I will be with them till the end.
And speaking of the charge of prayer
and confusion that surrounds,
the after, inner, outer lives,
I believe all interwound.
Faith, precept, ideology,
you choose what to call,
all my beliefs which I keep
betwixt in pending halls.
Here we must wade
across the intertwining streams
that meld together my so-called
"reality" and "dreams."
You see this red and fiery place?
Hither fear and anger lurk.
Yet upon a closer look you'll see
it's just a façade for more hurt.
As we move along
the images you see
are only recollections
of fading memories.
Laughter, weeping, sorrow, joy,
all things that come to pass,
bring about our composition,
but here we are, at last.
Alas we've reached the final stop
though we haven't traveled far,
and now the most essential part
of my intimate regard.
For all the exploits taken in
reckoned up, still not enough
to be as if a speck of dust
to my greatest asset…love.
I hope you did enjoy this venture
though I trust you think it strange.
Return at any time you wish
for tomorrow this all may change.

Tony Manfetano

You Changed My World

How do I start to breathe?
I need to release these words within me
Almighty and powerful
Your hand that changes my world
Spin me around
Can't let my feet touch this ground
Everywhere and every day
I am reminded of Your beauty
of Your touch
Because of You, oh God
I'm lost in Your arms
My life is secure
Far, so far away
I can see my troubles calling
They look and search for me
I just smile
because I have found a better place
I find existence and meaning
More love and devotion
A rain of blessings
Honor and sacrifice
Kneeling here in Your presence
This mountain, these waves, the silent moon
All speak and shout praises
Unheard praises
Beneath the heavens I am just a vessel
Almighty and powerful God
May I be a candlelight in your world

Monica Flores

Welcome to My Home

Given to everyone who visits my home

Welcome, welcome to my humble home,
Welcome to where the feline roam.
Where you must remove your shoes; leave the germs at the door,
Where rustic ambiance surrounds you, and live plants are galore.
Where the fresh air blows from room to room,
Where the mockingbirds sing much too soon, before the sun rises
majestically in the east,
Where fresh fruits and veggie announces a feast,
Where spices, fruits and smoothies dominate,
Because you are what you eat, and what you mastigate.
Where improvision notes dance with attitude and sazzz,
Where Miles, Coltrane, Brubeck re-invents bars of jazz.
Where lights are low because the computer reigns,
Where tap, tap, tap of the keys, compete with summer rains,
Where my terrace embraces and brags of its view,
Where the canal coexists with egrets, storks, equanas and ducks too!
Where the frogs and the crickets serenade against the evening sky,
Where mosquitoes buzz and dragon flies gracefully fly,
But home sweet home will settle in your bones,
Where incense burns from sticks, rocks, oils and cones,
Where frankincense and myrrh finds comfort in your nose,
While it clings to the ceiling and permeates your clothes,
Where unfinished projects never have a holiday,
Where there is meditation, yoga, chants and souls dare to pray,
Where windows are curtainless, yet embraces nature's daily gift,
Where the sun, moon, stars and clouds offer the soul's environ's lift,
Welcome, welcome to where the feline roam,
You are welcome, welcome to my humble home.

Penelope Alleyne

Growing Old with You

It all began about 60 years ago,
On a very special summers day,
For two unexpected teenage kids,
Love was about to come their way.

Boy meets girl, things move quick,
Nobody gave their love a chance,
It's been seen a million times before,
Just another hopeless young romance.

But for this couple it was different,
Since day one it was meant to be,
It was that forever fairytale happiness,
The kind you can only see on T.V.

One day she looked at him and asked,
"What is it with your life you'd like to do?"
He gently kissed her forehead and said,
"Sweetheart, I dream to grow old with you"

Smiling because they were so in love,
Suddenly he got down on one knee,
Pulled out a beautiful diamond ring,
And asked "Princess, will you marry me?"

Tears falling from her big brown eyes,
It was a yes as she nodded her head,
And just seven short months later,
These two teenage kids were wed.

They bought a house and settled down,
Got pregnant and gave birth to a little girl,
How is it at just twenty-three years old,
They could have everything in the world.

For fifty years their lives were perfect,
As grandchildren grew the love did too,
But with a simple trip to the doctor,
The future suddenly held a different view.

He was diagnosed with bone cancer,
The doctors didn't give him very long,
He fought with everything he had left,
But at eighty, he wasn't very strong.

As he lay in a hospital bed about to die,
Hand in hand with his best friend and wife,
He said "I want you to know since Nineteen,
You've been my everything, my whole life"

With tears falling from her big brown eyes,
She asked "did all of your dreams come true?"
He kissed her forehead and with his final breath,
Said "Of course princess, I grew old with you"

Courtney Holland

The Cry of a Twelve-Year-Old

The cry of a twelve-year-old....
The fear of inappropriate words said to me from a man so old.
Should I be frightened? Should I be scared? Will this man hurt me?
I thought to myself, no, my father couldn't hurt me,
that's just not the way it's supposed to be.
It's something I never visualized, I guess it took the experience to
    realize.
Honestly, it's something I thought my father could never do.
I felt so awful, so unclean. I took about ten showers that traumatic
    night.
I felt so disgusted, I couldn't believe
that the man who was supposed to love and protect me, my father,
is the man who hurt and raped me.

Jennifer Barela

Taylor's Dream

She takes a deep breath as she walks through the doors.
The young girl makes her way to the lunch table.
She finally takes a seat.
Everyone quickly scurries away.
She is left there feeling lonely, unwanted.
The only thing she looks forward to is
Going home and writing music.
People think she is weird for having a dream,
For wanting to be something,
When in reality, all she is
Is fearless.

The same girl walks through a town.
Guitar in hand, she walks into an office.
"Hi, my name's Taylor, I'm 11. Can I have a record deal?"
She constantly gets put down
But she still tries her hardest.
She comes home sad.
The girl sits down, plays guitar for hours.
Even though she hasn't succeeded,
She is still strong.

The same girl raises up from stage.
Thousands are screaming her name.
Taylor! Taylor! they yell.
The spotlight goes on her face.
As she starts strumming her guitar,
The audience stares in awe at her captivating blue eyes.
She starts to sing and the crowd goes wild.
"I don't think you should wait, I think you should
speak now."

A girl sits at the concert, tears in her eyes.
"Taylor I love you!" she screams.
Even though Taylor is far away, she still reaches out,
Hoping someday they will meet.
The girl sings along to every song, hoping Taylor will notice her.
As the last song is sung, Taylor gets on a balcony.
The balcony soars through the sky, glitter starts to rain on the audience.
The girl tries to catch glitter as Taylor floats above the crowd.
She looks up again, Taylor waves at her.
A piece of glitter floats into the palm of her hand.
She is overwhelmed with happiness.
The girl is breathless as Taylor's balcony sets down on the stage.
That girl is me.

Kayla Plater

Worship

W hich direction forward
O nward to
R aise your heart in love
S ilence before and
H opeful at peace
I n Jesus'
P lace of rest
Worship

Janice Richardson Hull

Jesus, Won't You Come?

I was singing, happy unto you, singing joy and rhythm too.
My world was perfect then, to myself and free of sin.
No one, I thought, could ever come in to steal what you had put within.
How'd I get here? I don't know.
I'm bleeding now, my world is dark.
The enemy came and stole my spark.
I cannot move, I feel unglued;
shattered now, I feel quite blue.
Spinning, anger and hate I should feel.
No one to cry to my only plea.
Jesus, do you still love me?
How could the enemy tread on me?
My world is now crashing down.
I feel completely, so unwound.
Alone I am in pain I stand.
No one knows the way I feel, the things they do are so unreal.
They know not they stab my heart.
They use my Lord and with everything I give, they depart,
taking and tearing of my heart.
Where is God? I'm crying out.
Can't He hear my screams and shout?
When, Lord, will they stop?
How many tears before this stops?
The day is long, the night is sharp;
visions come to break my heart.
I cry in pain and sleep not still.
Jesus, why am I still here?
When will you begin to heal?
Why must love not be real?
They sing and amuse you with the word, but cold is their heart, when
lies depart.

They only use me to play their part, God, but you know their heart.
Jesus, I'm bleeding, I want to come home,
feel Your embrace, Your loving arms.
This world no more can I face,
lift me up to Heaven's gate to enter in to see Your face.
There I shall not run and hide, no more thorns to hurt my side.
No longer my heart I will have to hide.
I wanna go I wanna come, Lord, keep me, please, from this gun.
I know You know I feel undone.
Nowhere is there for me to run.
Please now, Jesus, won't You come?

Colette Boudreaux

Into the Night

The stars shine so brightly here,
Here, where the skies are clear,
And no branches conceal the moon,
And no shadows stumble along the grass.

The stars shine so brightly here,
Away from all doubts and fear.
The wind whispers in the night,
Laughter dancing with the breeze.

The stars shine so brightly here
In a place with not a tear.
The music of the night sings
A gentle melody that calls to me.

Calling, calling, calling...
Dare I answer, and give way to this longing,
Step out from these trees,
Spread my wings and take flight?

Calling, calling, calling...
I feel like I should be crying.
This beauty is far too much for me;
So strange, it can't be real.

Calling, calling, calling...
I just can't escape this yearning.
One foot first, then the other,
Leaving my past far behind me.

I spread my wings with delight
From the forest into the night.

Hollie Hopson

The Stained Glass

They stare in unison
front and center
as the sun begins to rise

They close their eyes
and squeeze their hands
hoping someone listens

Hoping to hear a response
from someone who may not be there
But still they pray

They ask Him for forgiveness
and expect innocence to radiate
from their bodies like candlelight

As they stare up to the stained glass,
the cross, and his molded body stretched across it,
I wonder if anyone actually hears him,
if anyone actually believes,
if we are all are pretending to be something we're not.

Jordan Hayes

The Butcher

Cut me down the middle slice through, rip through
Watch the fear flow warm and obsolete
Dig deeper into the soul each unrelenting hack
Tears me down as I watch my own pain
An undeserving victim of an unaware assailant
The martyr I am, the murderer you are.
No conscience for you actions, have mine instead
Remedy your pain upon me, take out what you wish
Feast upon my willingness, a meal for a king or a queen.
Utilize my confidence to quell your inhibitions
Dominant, infinite, meaningless, it is to your liking.
Certain as uncertainty, and cold as stone inside
Drain me, Take all desired, communicate and dislocate
To you one and the same as you rape me from afar.
Captivate my refuge to reap the harvest
Of my shackled heart.
Enslaved in what I feel
My passion, your disdain
Unknowing yet again
I see you raise the knife
Raise the dagger of my own
Ripping out my insides
With the weakness I have honed
Turn away, walk away
And let me piece myself together
Scrambled like a jigsaw puzzle
I search myself to reassemble
Put it back the way I used to be
Or discover something different.

Bryce Willis

On Heaven's Doorstep

Bare feet on a
cool marble surface
Goose bumps appearing as
a cold wind passes by
Unfeeling, garish light
engulfs him
He shivers but his
clothes feel warm in the sun
Headaches and black dots
make him dizzy
An arm coils around his
waist, hoisting him up
A hooded man smiles at
him under a veil of stars
They ascend up the
smooth-surfaced stairs
The hooded man drags a heavy stick
behind him
The fallen angel at his left
his lifeless companion at his right

Slowly, the light breathes life
and the air becomes warm again
As they reach the head of the stairs
and face the golden woman Destiny

Heaven opens herself up to them
as soft cotton brushes against dirty skin
and pale feathers tickle the man's face

Shawnetta Lin Williams

Time

Some trees are gone, some houses changed
The years go by, there are new faces and names.
Things are different, obstacles are tackled down
What seemed so frightening is now as familiar as a drive-through
town.
It took me this long to understand what they meant,
but now growing up really does make sense.
There's always a challenge, some we can't face alone,
but what doesn't kill us makes us stronger and stronger we've grown.
From the smiles that made our teeth hurt, to the tears that drained our
eyes
Somehow we've made it through, after all these years we're still very
much alive.
From the early November frost to the late summer days,
time goes by fast and soon I'll be on my way.

Julia Buyak

A Rose That Was Coming into Bloom

A rose that was coming into bloom,
Its existence was taken too soon.
On the brink of greatness,
Your life wasn't faithless.
Your strength is in your belief,
Your smile provided relief.
Future was so bright,
This can't be right.
Your spirit is strong,
You're an angel that didn't stay long.
You are now in God's hands,
And he has some new plans.
Your soul has come into bloom,
But your existence was taken too soon.

Troy Charlton

This particular piece of poetry was written in memory of a family friend who had lost his life in an unfortunate accident. Poetry is a wonderful outlet for myself and others to pour out their emotions in a constructive way.

The Greatest Artist

The greatest artist of them all
Chooses to remain unknown—
Looking at abstract paintings down an infinite hall,
Sketched, intricately styled of my life that has grown.

He paints of beauty and remarkable sights
With a paintbrush pressed gently in His mighty hands—
A vivid painting is brought to life with different heights,
Vast, swaying sea and the promise of land.

The palette rests softly and still, offering various shades,
Hues of every color.
One can question, "Is it Heaven-made?"
Such an enormous task, our Creator endured.

Yet creating life, He once perfected,
But thoughts remain rejected, bodies still infected—
Diversity dissected,
Lives rushed and hectic.

In such a short time, we are allowed to breathe
Before the vicious claws grasp our death,
Until nothing but mere particles of time are left—
Such a ridiculous theft.

The greatest artist of them all
Wishes to remain unknown.
I reached the end of the infinite hall
And quietly watched my life grow.

Alexis Allen

21st Century Nursery Rhyme

Hey diddle diddle, Tiger Woods is a little
Off his game, and it's all due to sex.
When Mrs. Woods found
That he puttered around
She quickly became Tiger's ex!

Hey diddle diddle, here's a good riddle
What happened to golf's greatest star?
Though he can't seem to score
As he once did before,
His morals are way under par!

Jim Doney

Daddy's Dancing Boots

I bought steel-toed boots just for dancing; chocolate-brown with a
    black toe-cap.
They weren't made for a delicate prancing, or for ballet or jazz or for
    tap.
But they're perfect for me and for my little girl, as she grabs me with
    small eager hands,
Saying, "Daddy let's dance, one-two-three, turn and twirl!"
To a radio, record, or band.

She's a princess in gingham or denim or chintz, whether slippers,
    galoshes or clogs.
As she jumps on my toes, there is no need to wince; we're as graceful
    as kennel-show dogs.
Lucky me, dad will be, her first cotillion prince, and the first cheek
    she'll kiss—before frogs!

Often times she'll clomp in with them already on, with an impishly
    innocent smile.
She's the belle of the ball or the queen of the prom, with her fairy-
    tale, heroine style.
Once relinquished to me and a musical cue, then the boots strike
    their heroic pose.
Charming lad bows down low, to a curtsying lass; tiny feet climb
    atop of my toes.
We're the daddy-and-daughter, grand-ballroom revue, as we dance,
    one-two-three, turn and twirl.
Her gown flannel or fleece, coral green, coral blue, as her fuzzy pink
    slipper'd feet whirl.

We may one day sashay onto debutante tile, her bejeweled and
    begloved and begowned.
I'd be white-tied and tail'd with my steel-toed smile, as her Mary Janes
    glide without sound.
Our spontaneous "sock-hops" long proven worthwhile, with her feet
    never touching the ground.

On that first time we danced, I imagined the day we would dance with
    her dressed as a bride.
Adorned in organza, silk, lace and brocade, with her groom groomed
    and there by her side.
My formal wear may not need steel-toed boots, as I dance once again
    with my girl.
But we'll show all our timing was put to good use, as she'll reach to take
    hold of my hand,
Saying, "Daddy. Let's dance, one-two-three, turn and twirl."
Then we'll waltz to a grand wedding band.

I bought steel-toed boots just for dancing, chocolate-brown with a
    black toe-cap.
Sturdy work soles weren't put on for chancing, or a soft shoe, a plié, or
    tap.
But they're perfect for me and my little girl's girl, as she grabs me with
    small eager hands,
Saying, "Grandpa, let's dance! One-two-three, turn and twirl"
To a radio, record, or band.

Danny Boyle

Le Monde Est Cruel Et J'espfre Que Vous Planifits Dans Le Temps Pour L

I crave blood
Not to eat
Just to see
Seeping
Weeping
Take it from one who harms
Or the hero of the day
Taking from those who had begged
And having the forms of souls
Butterflies of silk fluttering
Calling you to the Eden
Of where you came
Singing your lullaby
Imagine
It's a world you created
Only for you
What would be in it?
What sights to behold?
Fountains?
Bridges?
Flower beds?
Music?
Waterfalls?
Animals?
What will you choose?
In your eyes the truth holds

Valeri Robles

Above the Influence

Trying to see a way
they light up,
killing brain cells,
destroying futures.
Pushing the goods,
push away
Good riddance.
You don't need
these aliens.
Abduction
of your brain;
flying above the sky
Earth
Universe
Out of here.
A shooting star:
shooting for the skies
but
ending in demise.
Above the influence
rather than out of your mind.

Allie Gremillion

Beautiful Earth Visions

An aqua-blue ocean engulfs the sun,
dolphins and seagulls playing so free.
   Seashells sparkle on the waterside sand,
this is where I've always dreamed to be.

   Flowing fields of the finest brown wheat,
flatlands for miles as far as you go.
   To jump from a barn into golden, sweet hay,
a happy time that I once did know.

   Mountains west with snow-capped peaks,
climb to the top and take a deep, heavenly breath.
   Majestic beauty lies in the valleys between,
a place to be buried at the time of my death.

   This new ocean will devour that same sun,
another place for me to laugh and play.
   Finally, I found somewhere I can be at peace,
I saw some beautiful earth visions today!

Amber Harris

Goodbye

Did you miss him at all when you said goodbye?
Did you shed any tears, begin to cry?
I wonder sometimes—what was going through your mind
When the separation became final, divorce papers signed?
But if your love can just stop, how did it even start?
They say it's not my fault, and you two grew apart
I know it didn't work, and though you two tried
The efforts just stopped—like a roller coaster ride

But now you are gone—out of my life
And I have moved on—much to this strife
If you were still with us, this would be a broken home
But instead you are missing; we've allowed you to roam
It's hard to think that you are gone forever
And it's hard to accept, even with as little as I remember

So goodbye to you, this pain you've left
You are *not* forgiven—that must be stressed
Even though I miss you and think of you often
It's you who left me, and my hatred won't soften
My life is now different, and the family has moved on
And though I wish you were here, I'm glad you're gone

Abby Grimes

Mind Race

Sometimes I feel that life is a race
that in order to win I must get first place.
I feel like a mouse who's stuck in a maze
that keeps hitting dead ends in a game of chase.
Whose clock am I on and why am I in a hurry?
Who's writing my life if this is my story?
Sometimes I forget to exhale and breathe
because life's like a treadmill that's under my feet.
Sometimes I run but mostly I fall
and after awhile I learn I can crawl.
At some point of exhaustion I crack up and laugh—
I've done so much running and I'm not on a track.
I remember the small things—the things taken for granted
and a smile takes form where it used to be slanted.
Who has you running and why run so fast
if we'll all cross the finish line…first…second or last?

Belinda Anaya

Pieta

A mother holds a folded flag;
The country's gift for loss of son.
She thinks of birth and baby days
To sounds of taps and crack of gun.
Enthused by flag and word he's sent
By those who want to get their way;
To win no matter what the cost to
Mother, sister, father, son.
She returns home in tears
To shrine of son forever gone.
A picture now in place of him,
Remembered as he was, unaged.

Donal Keohane

She Was Free

Staring onto the water
Cool breeze in her hair
She starts to sway to the rhythm
The ocean has created to share
She walks down the pier
Shedding her clothes as she goes
Till she's left with nothing
But her bare skin and long blonde hair
She doesn't pay notice
To the few people staring
Wondering if they should be concerned
She just keeps swaying
Then she reaches the edge
She climbs up on the railing
She lifts her arms up as far as she can
Takes a deep breath
Then dives
Deep into the ocean
Until her lungs can't take anymore
She floats back up to the surface
Swims her way to the ocean's edge
Lays down on the sand
Her naked skin exposed
She smiles
Then gets up
Finds her clothes
And moves along
No one ever saw that girl again
But she was never forgotten

Kayla Johnson

Love Letter to a Friend

I'm writing this letter to get this off my mind;
I've held it in long enough and have choked time after time.
I sit alone in my room at night and fantasize about "me and you."
Then I see you with others and my heart breaks into two.
I follow you with my eyes as casually you stroll by
And with that casual stroll comes only a meager "Hi."
Every time the phone rings I jump with electricity
Only to find it's not you calling for me.
I dream of you every night and think of you every day,
Hoping beyond all hopes that by chance you might send a glance my
    way.
The day always seems gloomier when you are not around me,
But when you are, it's like the calming of the stormiest sea.
To hear your voice is like smelling the first flowers of May.
To see you sends a feeling like hearing Liberace play.
I wish I could whisper to you all that I hold inside,
But you don't know that I exist, let alone what's on my mind.
Oh, what I would give to share the rest of your life.
How happy I would be for just an hour of your time!
We would invent new places only dreamed in the imaginations of man.
I'd take you to distant worlds; we'd explore uncharted land.
I'd give to you my mind, my heart, all my love 'til the end.
Until that day comes, though, this is a love letter from a friend.

Danitra Branch

Pain

It's empty, a shadow of what is now gone
It haunts you, the mem'ry, so twisted and wrong
A part of you lost, yourself torn apart
A gap in your life, a hole in your heart
You watch it, the darkness, it smolders and churns
What filled it has gone and never returns
You're lacking, so lifeless, so desperate to fill
And you're only breathing by sheer force of will
But then something fills you, that gap in your soul
A blanket, a whisper, to make you feel whole
It's pain; it's alive, it grows and it follows
It sneaks in your weakness and fills up your hollows
It comforts, a weight that now rests on your shoulder
It freezes like ice and makes you grow colder
It's light and you're blinded by bright shining day
It whispers so softly and whisks you away
Sometimes you fight it and keep strong your mind
But pain is a ghost that sneaks up from behind
It breaks you, it builds you, you can't see it come
Attacks you at midnight and then it goes numb
You're crushed and you're drowning you're living on tears
Your clothing is sorrow your shelter is fears
You're dying so slowly for gaps in your soul
And pain, though it kills you, makes everything whole
Its ease and completion, your very best friend
It fills up the gaping, the hole without end

Ashley Baker

A Hallow's Night

Where are the sounds?
Wet and cold outside...again
groups of less timid wander—some run.
Parents are far more frightened than their little ones.
Some shuttle their small cartoons and little monsters in
bright-eyed iron—steam and smoke rising.
But there once was another code
by foot only, I remember

The inside of my mask is wet
my breath
shouldn't there be more sound?
No, don't bother, their light is dimmed.

They start too early in the day
it's a sin to walk by sunlight
everyone knows that ghouls are creatures of the night.

But the smallest are first to arrive
by parents whose imaginations run wild.

Stephen Dake

Look to Me

Look to Me when times get rough.
Look to Me, child, give me your love.
Lift your head, child, when you see a block.
Lift your head, child, I am the rock.
Look to Me, child, when things aren't apparent.
Lift your head, child, I'll make things transparent.
Lift your head, child, they call me the Father, but you can call me Dad.
Look to Me, child, when times get rough and you're sad.
Lift your head, child, I want to make you Mine.
Look to Me, child, I won't leave you behind.

Michelle A. King

October Frights

October is when the wind howls,
rattling every bone.
October is when the nightmares
are free to roam and roam.
October is when the pumpkins live,
grinning their evil grins,
when the witches and the mummies
are free to commit their sins.
October is when the spirits
roam in the velvety black night.
October is when you'd better watch out
for a creepy October fright!

Ava Couchon

A Husband's Prayer

May God reach down from Heaven
And place His touch upon you
May you feel His special blessing
In everything that you do

May He place His hands upon your head
And bring good thoughts to your mind
May He place His hands upon your mouth
So your words will be true and kind

May He place His hands upon your ears
So that no sounds may offend you
May He place His hands upon your eyes
So His vision will live within you

May He place His hands upon your arms
With great power from above
May He place His hands upon your heart
And fill it with His love

May He place His hands upon your back
So that you stand straight and true
May He place His hands upon your legs
So you may walk in life anew

May He place hands upon your feet
To carry His love far and wide
May He place His hands upon your soul
And may He always be by your side

Tim Conaway

real life

she has all the chances in the world but her mind is to swirled into
    many pieces from this life
one soul handed her a knife but she doesn't know how to use it to
    protect herself
but that's enough to trouble oneself
there is no true direction and doesn't know where to go from where she
    is
now the only thing she wants is bliss and that one movie romantic kiss
the people say she has the world at her feet but she's running in place
the only thing she truly wants is to leave without a trace
but with that honest heart it makes it so hard to do that
so in return she just became a pack rat
to all the past memories that he refuses to let go
but with all the darkness that comes with every night she forces her
    mind to lie low
it never works the way she wants though
people say she has all the chances in the world but she will never
    believe in them
she just needs to learn how to use that knife and welcome herself to the
    real life

Ashley Brunmaier

A New Inspiration (Christina Perri)

A beautiful baby born on August 19th,
Her first cries so soft,
And her cries so sweet.
Those cries turned to words of ... inspiration!
A wonderful marriage started so fast and quick,
But her love didn't last divorce hit way too quick.
Her songs saved your life and everyone started listening!
You picked up as fast as a blue bird in flight,
 A new love of music came and it
Made you alright
I hope that you see that you're loved and you're safe,
Your family will always be close to your heart.
And now I hope that you hear my voice,
Outta all music you are my favorite choice.
P.S. You helped me get through my Aunt Shay's death and I hope that
    you know that your music means a lot to me.

Tiana Mohammed

Searching Inside

Searching inside I found unanswered goals and neglect
Searching deeper inside I found discrimination and regret
It was dark and desolate inside these chambers
Slowly I felt my way around

As I slowly searched inside I could feel the obstacle of fear
The walls of separation and whispers of defeat in my ear
Chills and stones of depression signaling the end is near

As I felt my way around I slipped and fell
Falling deeper and deeper

I suddenly fell on what felt like soft feathered pillows
I picked myself up and dusted myself off
As I looked around I could feel positiveness in the air

Above my head was the word success
Across my chest was the word potential
Below my feet was the word access

I took a deep breath
Savoring the feeling of peacefulness all around me
I suddenly realized that I was lost deep inside my soul

So I gathered my success
I gathered my potential
I picked up my access

I realized that I had to return them from within my soul
To receive the benefits of life

Roy Jackson Sr.

Live, Laugh and Love Forever

Life on this earth is not permanent,
Life on this earth is not easy,
Life on this earth is not a dream...

But how come we hold on to it so hard?
How come we can't see our life may end in the near future?
How come we think we will live forever?

We hold on because we love life,
We never see our life ending because we love our friends and family too
    much to ever let go.
We plan on living forever because we can never see what will happen
    next.

But life is short, life is hard and it's reality.
The only thing we can do to make it all better is:
Live well
Laugh often and
Love much...to make sure each moment counts.

Inna Svirgun

The Wonderful Works of Spring

As I walked through the woods today,
my heart began to sing,
for all around me I could see
the wonderful works of spring.

I saw a robin build her nest,
I heard cool waters flow,
the sunshine beamed from bluest skies
from which March winds did blow.

My dog walked proudly by my side
then ran ahead of me,
she chased the birds to watch them fly,
'twas quite a sight to see.

I felt the hand of God touch mine,
I heard the church bells ring.
I knew then He was showing me
the wonderful works of spring.

Margaret Stevenson

Fall

Leaves are falling all around;
frost appears out on the ground.
The harvest moon is a sight to see,
cool winds blowing through the trees.

Fall is here and what a treat;
summer is gone with great relief.
Time for planning a hayride or two,
then Thanksgiving and fall is through.

Not long 'til Old Man Winter unfolds;
we welcome the snow but not the cold.
Then before we know it, spring is here,
flowers blooming everywhere.

Summer is coming to sing its song;
we'd better get ready, it won't be long.
I don't mind to bear the heat
'cause fall is coming and what a treat!

Dianne Shaw

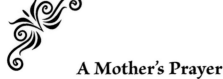

A Mother's Prayer

I held your hand when you were small,
I helped you up when you did fall.
I dried the tears from your saddened eyes
And brightened your outlook to the skies.

I taught you God's word, truth, and love
And watched you grow with his strength from above.
I said a silent prayer to God each night
That you would stay safe, snug, and tight.

And as you grew into a mother too,
I saw you pick up your child and coo,
Soothing words that calmed your child,
That made me happy and made me smile.

Silently I wait to hear
Those precious words so wonderful, so dear.
I understand, and I'm doing those things
That you taught me, mother, and I bring
Words of joy, happiness, and love
To my children from our Father above.

With understanding comes its reward,
Eternal life with our precious Lord.
But we must teach our children the way of life
So that they know and love the one true Christ.

For Christ alone can take our sin
To the Father He loves, and there it begins.
Our path unto forgiveness and eternal life,
With God the Father as our constant light.

A Mother's prayer is a simple one,
Love God and keep Him alone
In your heart so that your children will say,
I understand, and I will do it His way.
Only then will you gain eternal life
And understand the end of this world's strife.

Patty Scott

A Love Affair

I remember when our love affair started,
I was about 5 years old and I wrote about you on pieces of paper.
I didn't really know you then, though, so I had forgotten about you for
quite some time.
My love for you had faded until one day, when I was about 12 it was
re-struck and then I knew you and I'd known then that I'd have to have
you
But I don't think you felt the same way
Because I once again forgot about you
And once again at 14 I finally knew we were right for one another
Because you reminded me of my past love called music and showed me
that he was in you
You showed me that you weren't so different from a former friend
named Melody, nor a book called rap, nor a lover called Beat, or my
past love music at all
You showed me how to be myself and gave me my voice and how to
love who I am and what I do
And that's when I knew our love affair was meant to be, and it's all
because of you.

Alexa Cleveland

Distance

Distance
The great divider
Technology
The great deliverer

Together hearts as one, navigate
This uncharted fate
As we collaborate
And plan, our hearts await

With joy we live
Knowing each one cares
And a bounty fares
With sweetness each word spoken
To the heart an immeasurable token

So with willing souls
Distance does not feral
It is subdued with mighty sword
And taught not to underscore

For that which is in the heart
May be from the very start
Melodious to the soul
That love may unroll

In the mist and widespread day
May you carry me on your way
And in your thoughts, rest
For love blooms sweetly

Leann Brekke

I wrote this poem for my love Mark Vance, the finest man I've ever met

Me Without You

The tragedy was so soon, I had no clue
That there was no time left no one knew.
So my arms still ache to touch you once more.
To wrap them around you and hold you like before.
I yearn to hear your little voice too,
Mostly saying, "Mommy I love you."
I want to see you laugh and play,
To hear the funny things you liked to say.
Now I am left to dream of your beautiful face
Waking to nothing, empty space.
My arms reaching, grasping air,
For you are not really there.
Haunted by the life I knew,
This is me without you.

Crystal Birt

Soar

I stretch,
Wind beneath my wings.
I rotate my wings forward.
I flap.
Wind ruffles my feathers.
I'm off,
Soaring!
I'm parallel to the tree tops,
The leaves a dark emerald.
Castles of cloud drag above me.
All around the world is pure.
I slow.
I descend.
I stop flapping.
I've landed.
I remember my flight
And want to soar again.

Nicole Gauvreau

Secrets in the Trees

The trees,
they hold no judging eyes,
no hatred,
no stereotypes,
and no religious threats
of hell-ridden pathways for sinners like us.
I am not ashamed,
but afraid.
Society's love is only black or white
never in between,
so we consummate amid the woods.
The trees, they scream my name
as loud as you do, my love
and the echo resounds
reminding me of every last cry that escaped my lips,
but went unheard from the world.
It's our secret.
The bark sheds the sexual brown skin I'm in
with every stroke of friction
backs scarred
scarlet wounds
becoming one with my roots
of the African seas and drums
your ancestors took us from.
Centuries later
our hearts beat equally as one.
Histories collide in the middle of my thighs
of these forbidden pleasures
in pussy willows of mine
secrete and fertilize
unity in the form of mulattos.
Despite the racist whispers of our past
we are bound in the eyes of nature
and given the blessings of the earth.

Carrol Tibbs

Autumnal Equinox

Our days are getting shorter now,
But still our flowers grow.
So soon the frost puts them to sleep,
And they'll be under snow.

Although our air and sun are warm,
Our seasons we do trust.
On tops of mountains by our town
Is termination dust.

Fall's the time of color walks
When friendships deepen more,
We fantasize romantic talks
On warm, far distant shore.

The nights are getting longer now,
'Neath quilts we cuddle cool.
Now we have more time to play,
The children are in school.

And after work we can go ski,
So pleasant after dark,
While gliding down the lighted trails
We find in sparkling park.

Some can go out into crisp air
And have a hunting time.
While others sit by cozy fire
At home to write a rhyme.

On first Fridays we just go out
To see what artists do.
But there with care we are refreshed
And make a friend or two.

Then in winter solstice time,
We sit by roaring fire
With poems outside in winter's clime
Each other we inspire.

Break out our hospitality,
It's fun and joy to do.

We party when it's late until
We welcome year so new.

We go to see the Northern Lights,
And there we wonder why
So many planets and stars bright
Do share with us our sky.

There are great shows and music fine
With after parties too,
Where friends can kid each other well
Until their day is through.

For then we hold Fur Rendezvous
Where many show their ken.
Our special show of Anchorage
in cities' fairs top ten.

We drive out to a frozen lake
To watch the race cars go.
Will that one miss its skidding turn
And wind up in the snow?

In that great race across the state,
Those brave ones pray to God.
To food and dogs they do relate
To win Iditarod.

There are the weekend ev'nings
And on them we can go
To hear our friends reciting
In home and studio.

So do not mourn for summer time
Or for a change in weather.
Rejoice then for the season new
When we can be together.

Julius Rockwell Jr.

The Autumnal Equinox Party is held in the fall to celebrate the coming of winter to counteract depression that some have in anticipation of cold, short days and long nights in Alaska. Party attendees provide artistic encouragement. This poem sets the mood.

The Old Rugged Cross

The old rugged cross that
    stood so tall on that hill
The blood that was shed that day
    was oh, a terrible spill
There was no shame or loss
    in the face of the cross
The blood that stained the cross
    is a victory, not a loss
I love that old rugged cross
    where some say everything was a loss
To this old world the cross, you see
    is to hang a criminal of the earth with victory
The cross was carried with agony and pain
    to relieve the world of some of its shame
My attraction to this cross is more than they can see
    the Lord is holding out his hands to me
My treasures, they cannot ever see
    not of this earth, but oh, so heavenly
To the old rugged cross I will ever be true
    through the hurt and the pain, I'll always look to you
Until the day He calls me to my home far away
    I will always forgive and look the other way
To the home and treasures beyond belief
    to live with my Savior in great relief
So I'll cherish and love that old rugged cross
    for without it I am forever lost

Susan Wertz

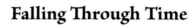

Falling Through Time

You have left me,
And now I am alone.
I think of you and I find myself
falling through time.
I fall back to the day we met
on Catalina Island, I can't forget
It was there we had our first kiss
the taste of your lips I do so miss
I am falling through time.
I remember the long walks we took by the sea
We were so happy then,
in love and so carefree!
I am falling through time.
I always remember
the way you used to look at me,
your eyes full of love
to last an eternity.
I am falling through time.
I remember your warm embrace
the look of love on your face.
Your smile was so disarming,
you were always so charming.
I am falling through time.
Sweetheart,
I have so many memories
you have left me,
even in my dreams
but they will always leave me
falling through time.
I fell in love with you so very long ago
and you were there to catch me.
Will you catch me as I am falling through time?

Denise Robertson

Time

Time carries its own scars
Each begin to fade every passing day
Some faster than others
Then there are those that embed themselves
Down to your psyche and latch on
Never to let go much to your chagrin
Every day you think, maybe today?
Then it hits you in your belly
Or right between the eyes
It doesn't play favorites anymore
Anything to bring you down
Eat away at your self-esteem
You try to think, what did I do?
Was it only one thing or an avalanche?
Picking up speed to bury you upon waking
Every morning as your eyes pop open
How do you handle rejection?
When it comes from within
It's not even verbalized anymore
It's a deep-rooted feeling
That keeps you grounded
To your own comfort zone of isolation

Barbara Cameron

Sleep Through the Storms

You toss and turn, you cannot sleep;
Then you hear the Father speak:
"Rest my child I am here
Go to sleep and have no fear.
Your Father God will take your storm;
I've been doing it since you were born.
When you accepted Me and first believed;
My helper and guide was then received.
Call on the Spirit to show you the way
Through any storm that comes today.
Bring your hurts, bring all your pain;
Give them to Me and your joy will remain.
I created the heavens and earth you see;
Nothing my child is impossible for Me.
I wait each day for you to come in prayer;
I look forward to what you have to share.
When you lost your loved ones...I cried;
When Satan said I didn't care...He lied!
They are safe with Me in a better place;
One day you too will see My face.
No one can love you the way that I do;
My love is unconditional, trusting and true.
Through all your storms I know what's best;
Call on Me, trust in Me, I will do the rest.
I can calm the storms of any sea;
I will calm the storms that rage in thee.
When you are hurting I am too;
Oh, how much I do love you."

Love, God

Carolyn Batchelder

We all go through storms in our lives, and when a dear friend was going through one, the Holy Spirit gave me this poem to encourage her, and I pray it will encourage everyone who reads it. Love in His grace, Carolyn Batchelder

The Leaves

A shimmer, a twinkle, a leaflet in wrinkle;
The sun has gilded the trees.
A glimmer, a flutter, and down comes another
To lie with the rest of the leaves.
So solemn, so wasteful, yet falling so graceful
To swerve and rock through the breeze,
Such beauty, such magic, but still oh so tragic
To die with the rest of the leaves.

Liam Shaw

I wrote this poem in 1985 for an assignment in twelfth grade English class. We were given random photos to write a story about. My photo was a silhouette of two leaves with the sun shining through between them. This is what emerged.

Prayer

Because in life I took the fast lane instead of taking my time and
enjoying the years as they came,
I decided to be dumb and not have a brain by not caring,
So I thought about catching the first train to entertain Satan by having
my faith slain,
Contemplating is my living in vain?

There were times when I felt patronized because in my mind I knew
what I was doing was wrong,
But I did it anyways because I knew You would forgive me later on.

When I chose to let go of Your hand,
Deciding to ignore Your ten commands because I wanted to follow my
own demands,
You still carried me leaving behind Your footprints in the sand,
Never leaving my side, with me You still stand,
Even when I turned my back, You forgave me right then.

When times got hard and I began to stress,
I started to confuse physical weariness with spiritual weakness,
But as my days go by I begin to realize that it's just a test,
Because You want me to apprehend Your doing of putting me down so
I can appreciate You bringing me up at my best

Donee Rayvonn Brown

Family Secrets

So many secrets kept to oneself...
I'm telling you,
But, shhh....don't tell.
Dad is out with her again,
Mom doesn't know...
So, shhh...don't tell.
Mom is drinking with her pills once again,
I saw her last night in the moon's bright light.
Dad doesn't know but last night she fell,
This is between you and I,
So shhh...don't tell.
Did you know brother never came home?
My sister says to each his own,
But it's only because she's now selling drugs.
She told me to help her hook my friends up.
I said it wouldn't happen, she pushed and shoved,
The gun to my head...
They never knew, never heard my yell.
I beg you, shhh...don't tell.
Me, well I'm all alone,
13 and pregnant, going through hell.
I was forced and raped...
But you're the only one I can tell.
Please don't cry,
And, shhh...don't tell.

Michelle Rodriguez

My poems are partly inspired by events from my own life. My poems are a way for me to vocalize my feelings and thoughts. My three children are a huge part of why I am able to transform difficult experiences in wonderful beauty.

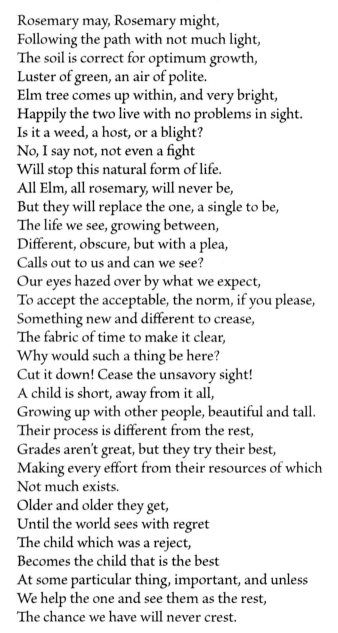

The Rose Elm

Rosemary may, Rosemary might,
Following the path with not much light,
The soil is correct for optimum growth,
Luster of green, an air of polite.
Elm tree comes up within, and very bright,
Happily the two live with no problems in sight.
Is it a weed, a host, or a blight?
No, I say not, not even a fight
Will stop this natural form of life.
All Elm, all rosemary, will never be,
But they will replace the one, a single to be,
The life we see, growing between,
Different, obscure, but with a plea,
Calls out to us and can we see?
Our eyes hazed over by what we expect,
To accept the acceptable, the norm, if you please,
Something new and different to crease,
The fabric of time to make it clear,
Why would such a thing be here?
Cut it down! Cease the unsavory sight!
A child is short, away from it all,
Growing up with other people, beautiful and tall.
Their process is different from the rest,
Grades aren't great, but they try their best,
Making every effort from their resources of which
Not much exists.
Older and older they get,
Until the world sees with regret
The child which was a reject,
Becomes the child that is the best
At some particular thing, important, and unless
We help the one and see them as the rest,
The chance we have will never crest.

Kenny Brackett

Day After Day

Day after day,
My love for you grows stronger.
Day after day,
I want to hold on to you longer and longer.
Day after day,
I get to see your beautiful smile.
Day after day,
I get to feel your soft kiss.
Day after day,
I get to embrace you in my arms.
Day after day,
I get to look into your gorgeous brown eyes.
And day after day,
I feel like the luckiest man alive!
I love you with all of my heart and always will,
Day after day.

Matt Wellwood

A Lighthouse of My Own

You're the beacon of light in the distance
Guiding me through life's most treacherous waters
Shedding light on the rocky shorelines that lie ahead
Steering me away from the wave-beaten caverns and coves
Revealing safe passage back to those whom I love
At the end of a long day's journey.

Anna Shepard

Daddy

Do you know how much I miss you, Daddy?
I'm pretty sure you don't.
I cry for the pain and shattered hearts,
But I cry for the loneliness too.

You don't know what you've done, Daddy.
I can't trust people anymore.
I'm not sure if someone will love me,
Then leave me in the cold.

What's it like where you are, Daddy,
In Phoenix with your new wife?
Do you know what I'm doing?
Do you even care?

I'll bet that you don't know, Daddy,
My favorite color, book, song.
You never cared to ask, Daddy,
Not like you were supposed to.

Sometimes it doesn't stop, Daddy,
The tears, the screams, the hurt.
I can't wash it all away
Like dirt, like mud, like blood.

Diana Sampson

As It Came Tapping

As it came pattering on my
Bedroom door, calling my name.
I lie, curled up
Under my cradle, wishing for the
Devilish thing to leave.

It continued tapping, the
Damn tapping never ending!
The creature never departing. My
Name came muffled through, calling
For the death of me.

I cover my ears, my head pounding
With the Scythe's drumming. I wasn't
Ready to be taken! Death was
Coming too soon! The wicked
Laughter continued calling.

The room spun with madness, sending
Me into a cocoon of darkness. But the
Beating became unceasing, becoming louder
And louder! Before it screamed into
My ears, making me shake with fear.

My body began to ache, slowly falling
Weak. The pattering finally stopped, but
It was too late. The thing crossed the threshold,
And it was unbeatable. It grabbed me
From my safe haven!

A spine-chilling shriek echoed,
Through the misty tavern. Blood
Splattered across the floor as the
Living thing held my beating heart. It had
Finally gotten me. I am forever now, no more.

Heidi Girdauckas

Oliver's Song

A lump in my throat, a tear in my eye
The doctor's stone face, the baby won't cry
No breath in his lungs, my heart skips a beat
For precious, fragile hands, for swollen, still feet

For little mouth so silent, such weight on my chest
Would trade all I have, and yet stand helpless
The panic, the fear, the sorrow and rage
Deepest despair, to this darkest stage

The seconds as hours, the minutes as days
I pray for solace, but agony stays
Then one tiny cough, one escape from death's grasp
And the world changed forever, for he made it at last

Kirk Heagle

Ode to Oprah

Oprah, the first 20 years of your show,
Of those years, there is not much that I know.
You were on, I was at work,
And this I did not shirk.
Then I retired, you see,
And crafty me,
I began to sew, quilt and knit
For charity, no time for TV to sit.
Then my life you awoke
When with Eckhart Tolle you spoke.
Your classes I took,
I still re-read the book.
Now in life classes I see your joy
Giving things big or small as a toy.
The Bible says it is better to give than receive.
I can see this is what you truly believe.
 "Keep up your giving it makes joyous living,
So live it and love it and make the most of it for life is a wonderful
    thing."
That is a quote from a record Sophie Tucker did sing.

Betty Shorten

Daybreak

Chill, frosted air, curl my toes and stomp my feet; parallel ebony wires
tie me to the bright heat rising.

Gasconading crows, shadows depart; my tuneless whistle grates and
boots aged with dust of the past shrink from that to come.

Dry baked heat; slap a fly, shaded face drawn to a lone chair on the
veranda.

Odours of fertility, rich coffee, joy of completion, Eden's breathing leads
me on.

Out of place, out-manoeuvred, a break in spirit; yet somewhere in the
basement, a guide needs to fulfil a complex promise.

Time to connect, strangers in passing, chuckles beginning, stories on
offer, ancient switchboards still chatter.

Strength and humour, gratitude bubbling; build shared joy and
creativity, not sorrow for mourning.

Dream weaving, new skills, rebirth, destiny yet distant, still to be
challenged. To Eden's beauty how can I not respond?

Robyn Freckelton

A Triumphant Defeat

Depression was created by man
You kill man, you kill depression
Tears were created by depression
You kill tears, you kill pain
Pain was created by death
You kill death, you kill sadness
Sadness is what fills my soul
You kill my soul, I am a lifeless doll
Dolls were created by man
You kill dolls, you kill happiness
Happiness is what I don't have
You kill man, you kill us all
Death causes depression
You kill me, sadness takes over
You're sad, I'm full of happiness
I'm full of happiness, who needs dolls
You kill the creators of dolls
You kill man
You kill man
I smile in triumph

Madelaine Sarah Allison

Nine Lives

Nine lives
flowing nine ways
with every life
flowing one way
nine lives
running nine miles
while giving a life
to every mile
nine lives
fetching many tunes
from many flow
with each flow
running through
every mile with a song

Olakunle Campbell

Sweet Flowers

I sit here in our meadow
thinking and dreaming of how it was
and could have been

I look around our meadow
it's destroyed, dark, and gloomy
as if it knows how I feel

I breathe in our meadow
it has lost us and its magic
It screams hell

We have changed in our meadow
and know everything
all too well

The grass knows
that every day
we lay on our backs staring at the sun

The wind knows
every word
even the ones you whispered slowly in my ear

The flowers know
every time
you lifted my chin to gently kiss me

And the rain now knows
every tear
that fell down my porcelain face

The world caved in now
my head spinning
the ground crumbling beneath me

And before everything
went black I smelled
the fragrance of sweet flowers

Vanessa Barraco

This poem was an entry in my journal for a grade twelve creative writing course. I am a figure skater and my poem was inspired by a song I skated to called, "Fields of Gold," by Eva Cassidy, use of pastoral setting for a love story.

Hoping for You

Sometimes I feel as though I could miss you
Like you were once upon a time my best friend
And I don't even know you
But I want to, I will
It takes my breath away
Every time I think how close I was to you
If I ran so hard, so fast
If I met you
Nothing could take away
The high I would've had from you
And my fingers ache
To tangle through your curls
And my palms tingle with the want
To bring your face to mine
My arms reach out to try and catch you
My body warms, my heart soars
My smile brightens
At just the thought of you
You're perfect to me
I'm in love with who I believe that you are

Juliana Krouse

Luna

Luna clung to the bark of the trees
When the beats of the bees and cattails ceased
Among the resting flora and fauna,
Its wings kissed by the northern aurora.
Its soft downy scales float with an ease
Among cherry blossom petals in the breeze.
But above the canopy, the demon hovers.
Summer nights chill, the forest shudders.
Wind fills the linen sails
Between the bony fingers and nails.
The furrowed body surfs the gale,
Tongue longing for the tang of sweet innocence,
The demon emitting waves of malevolence.
Luna finds strength, the velvety beauty takes flight,
Soaring to avoid her horrific plight.
To the willow and her beckoning branches,
Luna aims for the vines will all her intensions.
The demon flies
Luna dives
The nightingale sighs

Nicholas Ronk

If I Could Give You the World

If I could give you the world,
I would.

The sea would be all the love I have for you,
spreading out for miles.
The sky would be the happiness that surrounds you,
lighting up your smiles.

If I could give you the world,
I would.

The rain would be the tears you cry
from the laughter that can't be described,
like the greatest sound to the ear.

If I could give you the world,
I would.

Dara DenDekker

Dad

We all knew the time would come, and we knew it was near
But we could not accept this and tried to look beyond the fear
The fear of losing you, Dad, someone so special and loved
But the time came and God took you to Heaven above
You were so young, Dad, it was too soon to say goodbye
And all we can do, Dad, is just ask why
Why did you have to go, Dad, why couldn't you stay?
Stay in our lives forever, Dad, to have you here each day?
But we were all there, Dad, by your side 'til the end
Knowing soon enough all your pains God would mend
We were there, Dad, as you took your last breath
And faded away from the living and into death
Away from our lives, but never our hearts
For even in death, our lives you will always be a part
For your family you have done so much
We feel we could never thank you enough
Everyone's hearts you have truly touched
And we will all miss you, Dad, forever, so very much

Mandie Kohlenberg

Girl

There she is, the girl that was doubted, the girl that was blamed.
You should feel ashamed, look at what you drove her to, she's gone
    insane.
The pain she's felt will never go away.
She did her best with everything in life. Yet that wasn't enough.
She always tried to please everyone, always put others before herself.
In the end, she had no one to call a friend.
She was left alone and didn't know why.
The heartache inside made her want to hide.
The reality left her paralyzed with tearing eyes.
Her pride has died because of your lies.
If you think you destroyed her you're wrong.
She's been a fighter all along.
Just so you know she's happy.
Now turn around and you'll see that girl is me.

Yohanna Bonilla

Home

Home is where the heart is,
But for me this isn't true,
If home is where the heart is,
Then why aren't I with you?

You came to me and fell in love,
And then you stole my heart,
Inside you it beats fast
Whenever we're apart!

You have mine and I have yours.
But I wish that you could see
Your home is right here,
Curled up next to me!

If you love me you'll come home
and take me into your arms
and sweep me away
in your sea full of charms!

Ashlee Cornelius

I Can't

You can see the real
me but not who I
want to be, can't help if
I want to be different
instead of who I am, I can't
help if you're the same as me.
I need to be what my destiny
wants me to be, I want to be
because my parents want
to know where I go and what I do
so I can't

Samantha Chandler

Mama Can't Hear Me

Mama, the baby's crying.
Mama, ain't no milk.
Mama, the TV won't work.
Mama, we're hungry.
Mama, ain't no food in the refrigerator.
Mama's in the room smoking that stuff,
I hope she buys some food tomorrow, it's check day.
Mama, ain't no soap, we can't take a bath.
Man, got up this morning picking through dirty clothes to go to school.
Ooh, some pizza from the night before,
Oh God, that means Paul is in there with her.
I hate him, he's always beating on her, don't see him 'till check day.
I hope she saves some money to wash with.
Mama, we're home.
Mama! The baby is crying!
I went into her room, she's lying in her own vomit.
Ma! Ma! Mama can't hear me. Mama's dead.

Frances Hurt

I have enjoyed writing for years. I always just write then throw it in my writer's file. I recently became ill and had to quit work. So being bored, I decided to submit a poem. Now I'm am glad that I did. I feel good about myself.

My Future

Can you see how much I'm falling for
you?
Is it showing in my eyes?
Can you tell by the things I do
or when I talk?
There is no way to conceal, what I'm
feeling for you now!
All I feel is real, you stole my heart
somehow!
The way you're so romantic,
you're sexy, and you're smart.
The way you tease with antics,
I love each and every part!
Your eyes can put me in a trance,
Your voice sweeter than an angel's
song.
All it takes is just one glance,
and I'm restless all night long.
You're my honey, my sweetie, my baby
and you know, you are my friend!
If I'm lucky, well then maybe we will
never end.

David Lynn Dees

My Missing Voice

You are so smart and kind,
To women you are a hard find,
To me you are truly one of a kind.
My life now is so much more,
Because you helped me open that door.
Before you came along,
My mind, my thoughts were almost all gone.
I had no hope,
My only plan was to elope.
I was scared and it seemed as if no one cared.
For a year I had no one near.
I had only one person who taught me the meaning of fear.
Broken down till I was no more,
I came back home, just to go to my room.
My life was my job, I could no longer sob.
I was a zombie with no feelings
But then I ran into a voice and by my own choice,
I stayed to investigate what I had found.
What I found had me running 'round and 'round.
I hope to find what I found again someday
Because your voice, your touch, your thoughts
Are all I have ever wanted.
But my mind is clouding up my heart.
I hope to not be apart from this voice for too long
Unless my mind has put my heart in the wrong.
You're my Savior who has brought me hope and taught me how to
    cope.
Thank you for coming to me and helping me see again.

Christin Thomson

My Name Is

My name is Milagros
It's a name I've never heard before
A Spanish word
In English it means miracle

I am from a country of independence
A land of freedom
A state of the rocky mountains
Where things aren't always as they seem

If I were an animal I would be a white tiger
Strong and powerful so no one would
Hurt me

If there were a word on my forehead
It would be next
Because I always wonder what's next
Anxious for life's next challenge

If my hands could speak
They would curse and curse
And wonder why I do the things I do

My favorite smell is of food cooking in the kitchen because it's
    my mom, safe
My least favorite smell is of sadness
Because it takes me back to all the sad times

My favorite memory is of spending time with my family
Because in the end that's all that matters

Milagros Rizo

Pieces of Our Lives

Pieces of words here and there,
We always excuse, forgive,
Done all the time, anywhere
And we continue, we outlive.

It causes hurt deep inside
Words reaching secret spaces,
Hence forgetting honor or pride
We see no sorrow on the faces.

Feelings kept, not shown
We don't give of ourselves,
But torn pieces of our own
Loneliness hidden in shelves.

Old stories, memories blown
Long-ago romances,
We know we are alone
Furious discontinuances.

Cascading tiers of our lives
Little pieces of our own,
So many remains of afterlives
Unfolding into the unknown.

Christina Daltro

Rumors

They say words don't hurt
But deep inside everyone knows they do
You feel crushed
Stuck with a never-ending migraine
Rumors ruin me
Misread hugs
Misread moments
No one understands how it makes me feel
Under the blanket is where I lay
Away from everyone today
You make me feel like crap
Like I'm stuck in a trap
I hate the lies that form
Misunderstood
The words that lie
I feel decayed
Gone inside
The only one alone
I hate being misunderstood
Know me better than that
My actions remain a rumor
Innocent hug for my tears
Got twisted into something worse
They say words don't hurt
But I know better

Brianna Newcomb

Someone Like You

You are my sky, my need to go above.
You are my friend, my need to have love.

You are my goal to be great then better,
You are like myself before I ever met her.

You are like my dad, protective, but lets go.
You are like my mom, filled with more compassion then I'll ever know.

You are like the good old days, chivalrous despite death.
You are like my heart, my mind, and my breath.

You are like everyone I love, need, and knew.
But you, no one is like you.

Miranda Smith

Steal the Night Away

I'm here to say hey, let's talk for a little while I know I never talk about how happy I am to see you I know my words are never about the butterflies of the day I never see rainbows and it rains down on me but oh baby if we ever touch I'd say...

Let's steal the night away like a shooting star we'll shine bright and the heavens above will gaze down on our light and sigh

I know I tell you about my fears and the scary dreams but you always give me a silver line to these dark clouds and the storms go away, I look inside my heart to find a word that I could use for you but I'm left speechless in my attempts to wow you I only have this to say...

Let's steal the night away like a shooting star we'll shine bright and the heavens above will gaze down on our light and sigh

I want to get it all off my chest maybe I'll be the only one left I'll live to be by your side bad sad or mad I'll try to give you the silver from my soul to shine up your day I know you have everything you already need but I'll be here if they vanish in thin air and I'll have this to say...

Let's steal the night away like a shooting star we'll shine bright and the heavens above will gaze down on our light and sigh

This is what I have to say I'll burn my inside to show you my light I hope you'll do the same and not blame I'll be good and not show you my shame I only have this to say...

Let's steal the night away like a shooting star we'll shine bright and the heavens above will gaze down on our light and sigh

Let's steal the night away and turn our passion into a light. Let's steal the night away and never say goodbye

Let's steal the night away and take the stars. Let's steal the night away Let's steal the night away this time

Oh I'd love to say, let's steal the night away

Justin Contreras

The Defenders

They are brothers, sisters, fathers, mothers.
These heroes fall for the freedoms of others.
They pack up their gear for trips to foreign land
To protect all Americans with weapon in hand.
Where they go they are hated and despised with disgusts
To protect this nation in God we trust.
They hunt down those who wish to put us under.
When in the fight their weapons do thunder.
They do it for patriotism and freedom for all.
It's sad to know that some will fall.
They miss time with family and friends.
If you ask them if they would, they'd do it again.
They don't do it for fame, fortune, or glory.
They do it for freedom, that's their story.
When you think of your freedom, when you see one, if you would.
Give thanks to the soldiers who gave all that they could.

Peter Warneck

Theatre of Tragedy

So now it's time to die
in this theatre of tragedy.
Close your eyes and end it all
in this theatre of tragedy.
We're all mindless puppets,
manipulated by love
in this tragedy.
We all want love,
but the world has run out
in this theatre of tragedy.
I will go there and find it myself,
or myself,
or me,
or possibly you.
I can't see past the tears,
the sweet sounds of my cries,
entertain an audience of a thousand.
My heart is as empty as the stage I share with you,
but we share nothing more than @#$% and hatred.
After all, we're living in a tragedy.
A tragic world filled with tragic souls and tragic people.
So I'll sing to the damned,
cry to the deaf,
and show the blind to love
in this theatre of tragedy.

Joey Hoffman

Time

Where do we come from? Where do we go?
What will be of tomorrow?
Moments that pass...memories that last
Times of happiness and sorrow

What becomes of this world? Will it keep moving on?
Will the waves always crash from the sea?
As I sit here in a daze...thinking life's one big maze
My thoughts wonder in curiosity

(Chorus) Time just keeps drifting by
Like a chime drifting in the wind that cannot ascend

So much to know...a long way to go
Living each day by the minute
So many faces...so many places
The world seems infinite

So tell me what is time? Just a passing cloud?
Or the lines of a weathered, worn face?
The sun has begone...won't rise until dawn
As I sit here and watch the world go on

Karen St. Claire

As president of VAMPLIFIED® "Amplified Vampire Rock," Karen St. Claire is a Hollywood based music composer, lyricist, recording artist, producer, and painter.

Waterfalls at Night

As the river that flows in different directions
Waterfalls at night were the only salvation
Streams of droplet strolling down a face
For the love of a heart that it could never embrace
Roaring waves enclosed in a shell as the whimpering sounds of a heart
    attempts to propel
A halo so bright that guides the direction into lagoons of pristine clear
    reflections

Arlene Santiago

Momma's Remedies

Sometimes when I reflect upon our lives back on the farm
I marvel at our mother who protected us from harm
She met each new emergency and handled all of these
She solved all our catastrophes and seemingly with ease

Whate'er the problem big or small Mom always had a plan
No rocket scientist needed here to lend a helping hand
No college education, no university
Was called upon for knowledge to help our family

Sulfur and molasses was a "cure all" at our place
And the daily tasty raisins kept those pimples off our face
Ginger cocktails waited steaming when we came in from a storm
And those mustard plasters for the croup were way more hot than
    warn

When pestilence came calling Momma had a cure for that
With simple things around the house and the help of old Tom cat
Sulfur killed the bedbugs coal oil killed the lice
DDT killed stinging things and cat killed all the mice

Everything was handled in the simplest of ways
No need for all the drama that we seem to need today

Elizabeth Renaud Aldred

*In 2003, I began writing my memoirs of my life on the farm (as I remember)
through the years 1937–1952. I now have over fifty poems in my album.
Momma's remedies are some of my most cherished memories of that time in my
life.*

What Is Poetry?

Poetry is not something you can touch, though it may touch you,
Like trying to grab a fistful of smoke.
Writing poetry is like trying to make sense of something Picasso drew,
Though through a strong emotion inspiration is provoked.
Poetry is a will to emulate life's wonder,
But it can never compare with God's creatures,
So through many a year we blunder,
Trying to feel the world from a piece of paper, as the beseechers.
Poetry tugs at the heart.
Some makes you want to laugh or cry.
I would say that is a good start
To making words come to life. And like the sweetest goodbye,
I say *adieu*, and let you ponder
Life's little wonders.

Kaeli Burkett

Eyes Meet

Eyes meet
Answering without sound
Wanting dripping like tears from sapphire
Longing to hold, to hug
Fear of resentment abstains
Distance forms a sheer black veil
Shielding thoughts
Avoiding questions
Muffled emotion screams unwanted
And I wait
Eyes searching head down in shame
Who stares at me with judgment in the silver glass
Wanting closure
Reaping no end
Bathed in the moonlight
Knowing you are doing the same

Tom St. Joseph

Monarch

He reaches over from his wooden seat
Cautious to make a move
Slowly slides to the right
to get closer to you
A single breath scares him away
and soon he is no longer there
He will be back soon
when the monarchs come back
on a warm July afternoon

Marlie Soderquist

So Far Away

Broken and ragged on the floor,
My mind jumbled,
All I could think of was you.

I thought of you,
All of your flaws,
Every little thing you do,
And it brought tears to my eyes.

I looked at my hands,
Dirty and empty,
And imagined your hands
Closing in around them.

You were so close to my heart,
Yet so far away,
I couldn't take it,
I couldn't just sit there
And let you escape my grasp.

I used the sliver of strength I had left
To get up off the floor,
Dust myself off,
And leave to find you,
So far away.

Kelly Schroeder

The Past

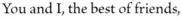

You and I, the best of friends,
Your mom was my mom and mine was yours.
We were inseparable!
I was at your house or you were at mine,
We were a package deal.
You would finish my sentence and I would know your thoughts.
Nothing could separate us, we were one.
People thought we were sisters,
And that's what we were, friends on the outside, sisters at heart.

But that's all in the past now,
No way to reverse time.
You left me, for no reason that I could see.
I tried to understand,
But it was a waste of time.
It just seemed like you didn't care anymore.
You found new friends very quickly,
For me . . . it took years.
You hurt me long ago.
But I have finally forgiven you.
However, I'll never forget that day,
The worst day of my life.

We were no longer best friends.
I didn't talk to your mom, and you didn't talk to mine.
We were never together.
I didn't go to your house and you didn't come to mine.
We were no longer a package deal.
We no longer knew what the other thought.
We were separate, no longer one.
You and I were not sisters anymore.
But now that's all in the past.

Jessica Baise

My poem, "The Past," was just a small glimpse into what became a big part of my life. This is just a small part of why I love poetry; it can let me express myself so much, but with so few words.

Imprisoned

Oh I never thought that I'd
I'd see in your eye
The thought of your betrayal
Or how you'd leave me here
I took a look at you
A look at you two
And I realized the pain
That I have held on to
I never thought we would
Never thought you could
Do this to me even now
After all we've been through
Now I am stuck
Within my own prison
You hold the key
And I can't pick the lock
Oh someone let me out
No one hears me shout
Someone let me out

Dylan Christopher

Sin and Death

Darkness now creeps from white-washed hands,
Black ink to blemish pale skin.
Watch it crawl and creep with life
And to all it touches doth come strife.

The darkness reaches deep within,
Grabbing hold of all life-giving,
And wrenches—pulls—without restraint
As we cry aloud in pain.

We writhe and moan as the accursed
Black ink now invades our systems,
wreaking havoc as it goes.
We cry yet louder as it burrows.

Feel it move into the heart
And rip the fragile flesh apart.
Bloodcurdling screams now fill the air
As blood pours from that wound there.

As we cry out, see him smile
Like Cheshire Cat as all the while
Master of darkness merely stalks
Those his ink hath yet to mark.

Those be they that ever live
Unaware of danger, and in bliss
Ignoring the darkness day by day
As if to keep the black ink at bay.

Leiland Arnholt

Ending

Soon your world comes crashing down
but the glass breaking won't make a sound
because once you're dead you can't feel the pain
eventually everyone finds someone else to blame

Cries can be heard in the dead of the night
people soon realize they no longer can fight
the knife digs much deeper each time it hits skin
maybe as the blood leaves, it'll wash away sin

Hunger soon strikes abandoned hearts
lies are what tore the whole world apart
deep in the graveyard, the dead sing their songs
hoping the depressed ones will sing along

my heart is so lost, so filled with fear
I begin to realize my ending is near
I'll be dead deep in the graveyard, singing my song
I've passed the part where I sing along

I will not hear the glass hit the ground
I will not feel the world spin around
the knife stabs my skin, but I won't feel the pain
for this is my death, and I've you to blame

Jennifer Bailey

Touch of Time

Tick tick tick tock,
I count the seconds on the clock.
Seconds, minutes, hours, days,
I watch all of the sun's rays.

Watch the rays fade with time,
Fade along with the rhyme.
Rhyme turns to rhythm then to beat,
The beat of my soul as I retreat.

Hear the beat, feel the breath,
We don't know how much time is left.
Need you, feel you, want you so,
Never want to let it go.

Your touch on my skin burns,
Everything starts to turn.
The room in spinning I cannot breathe,
This is all that I need.

Ariel Trost

War Till the End

When I ask, will it be enough?
When will greed and hate
Be placed aside to end this war?
Will we wait for us to kill ourselves?
So no one is here to run the world
And protect all that we have accomplished
Widows weep with tear-matted hair on their faces
Tightly embracing their men's shirts and cologne
Only to wallow in harsh memories
Cities covered in dirt and darkness
Along with blood-colored, rusted metal shells
With echoes of the many voices once there
The fields of a long-ago-loved land—forgotten
Vines killing trees, and weeds killing flowers
While starving predators kill all in sight
Cows scream in pain as they stagger
Their udders swollen and aching
With no one to help them release their burden
Food rotten and soon brings on famine
Children, hungry and thinned, beg their mothers for food
And with no men to put love in women's wombs, births are depleted
Pain brings on devastation, and whoever is left crumbles
No more children's laughter on lonely days
Cows permeate thick stink, as they rot in the sun
Heaps of metal litter the once fascinating streets
And the women still with limp sentimentals in hand
Their fingers gnarled and skin loosely grey; they still cling
In hopes that when they open their sunken eyes
It will all be a mistake that God fixed when he saw their grief.

Emily Feltz

break free

she watched the clouds go by,
she looked to god and asked him why.
the man with whom she'd fallen in love,
her heaven-sent angel from high up above,
couldn't see her tonight.
but she swore shed try not to cry.
but she's been done wrong far too long.
she'll have to break into the light.

she's gotta break out,
she's gotta break free
and get to a place where she's happy
a place to laugh, a place to love,
a place for her and her star above.
she's gotta break out, she's gotta break out.

the tears that well up in her eyes are threatening to fall
so she got down on her hands and knees
and let those teardrops fall.
she cried and cried till she could no more,
and the stars began to shine.
she took his hand right then and there,
and since then she hasn't cried.

she finally broke out,
she finally got free,
got to a place where she's happy
a place to laugh, a place to love,
a place for her and her star above.
she finally broke out.
she finally broke out. she finally got free.
she's in a place where she's happy.

Melissa Jordan

I Need You

When I say, "I need you"
I don't want to wonder if you'll ever come to my rescue
Or whether you'll leave me drowning in a pool of sorrow of your creation
Sick from the lack of communication that's been lost in translation
I have a high tolerance for understanding but that is far from limitless
So I trudge the narrow divide
Separated by the feelings I hide
I'm on the brink of a heart divided
As I piece together what's been broken
Searching to reunite what's been stolen
My heart has been constantly crushed fighting to stay alive
Still, I hold it in because of my pride
Lacking the strength to continue
Yet I still strive
I strive to be more than just an occupant of space
I strive to be your one true love so that no other man can take my place
I strive to be more than some dude you just live with
I strive to be the father of our children
And that includes the number you had when we started this
So if you want to lock me down and have the key, I'm down
Down to allow you to assume the role of wife
Let's make those life decisions to magnify our quality of life
All I ask is that you follow my lead as I refer to Langston Hughes
Hold fast to your dreams, there's nothing you can't do
Fly high and let nothing hold you back
Knowledge is key, not something you lack
Open your mind and discover new revelations
I need you to be greater
Be greater than your own expectations

Victor Breon Johnson

My Mother exposed me to poetry at an early age but never realized how big a part it would play in my life. It is a great honor to have my poem, "I Need You," published in this literary collection.

Faded Flowers

In all the flowers faded
I could not catch your face
They do not bring a time
I do not see a place

Once I dreamt a dream
When by golden skies I was blinded
But nightfall bought me clarity
That your closeness never will

In all the flowers faded
I'll never catch your face
You never had the time
You'll never have a place

Now I lay in silence and
I think upon the past
Here and now I wonder how
How can anything last

Once I dreamt a dream
When by golden skies I was blinded
Faded flowers gather dust
Nightfall brings a solitude I've never truly minded.

Shawna Crisler

Poison Ivy

Itching
Burning
Irritating
Poison Ivy on your skin
Festering
Boiling
It sears itself in your flesh.
It spreads up your arm,
creeping across your chest.
You wonder when you'll be fully consumed.
It burns a dark red
anger,
frustration,
as it reaches your hips.
Like wild fire it spreads
until you're fully covered.
It only took one touch,
one @#$% from the green plant,
one drop of the poisonous oil,
for you to be consumed.

Christopher Udal

Just a Wish

Take me away to a sacred place
Where no one or nothing can hear us.
Let's look at the sky.
Watch the stars—look, a shooting star!
Make a wish.
I have no wish but to let this moment last.

There's not a cloud in the sky,
There's a great breeze to make this
Night absolutely perfect.
Nothing could ruin this,
We are out in the open,
Some trees around but not many.
The city is miles away, so there are
Many more stars and they shine so bright.

There's no one around to tell us to leave,
We can do what we want.

Carli Taylor

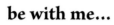

be with me...

awaken the phoenix
the angel inside
bring out what you see
when you look into my eyes
my soul is a fire
soft and without demise
few can see past my mask
and appreciate what's behind this guise
talented and powerful
destiny awaits
i am a child nervous and uncertain to move beyond the gates
hold my hand and help me through
blossom me like a rose, my love
your kisses carry me true
blossom me like the spring
as i'm falling for you
be with me my love
be with me till the end
your smile is my reward
our love is godsend
awaken the phoenix
and set your heart ablaze
i wrap my arms around you
launch off and fly away
be with me, my love
and never let me go
i send my heart with you
and wherever you may roam
be with me my love
this i whisper in your ear
words too deep to mention
secretly our own
and secretly love to hear

Erica Marie Horton

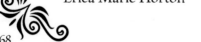

Secret Garden

The blindfold comes off
and I see your secret,
the dark force of your eyes
seems to pull me in
Something about your smile
makes my breath catch
and my soul chain itself tighter

The sights all around
combined with the sensation
of your arms around me
have my head spinning

Dead vines hanging from stone walls,
forgotten by history
Burnt, ashen rose bushes
ancient, knotted trees
their branches torn in all directions
tell of a love story gone dark
and yet, it's still beautiful

This secret garden,
time's own testament
history's forgotten
war-torn love story
of undying love
that destroyed everything

Suzannah Godwin

Do You See Them?

Do you see them with wild hair flying in the wind
and swords raised together shining in the sun?
Lifting their battle-weary eyes to Heaven,
they send a prayer for victory and sweet peace when day is done.
They line up, then charge forward as one man.
Sharp blades clash together loudly in the air,
as each brave man fights as well as he can.
To protect all his lands and family in his care,
some are all too soon struck down,
and their dreams die with them on the ground.
While others fight on and on, without any harm,
and the world keeps turning round and round.
And sunlight flickers across each field and farm.
Silently, the day slips into the night,
and the men are tired and sore and spent.
And many of them lay where fallen in the moonlight.
Their souls swiftly to the Maker are sent.
At battle's end, all that's left is the wind
and waving fields of grass,
stained with blood and tears shed for them.
Their weapons all stained with blood and tears of anguish at day's end,
only a few still stand sound of mind and limb.
Breathing deeply of the fresh, cool air stirring in the field,
the living retrieve each weapon, sword and shield.
Only one lone horse remains, waiting for his master,
As he strides across the grass looking for his fallen friends and foe.
He gives comfort to those who survived the disaster,
and bids farewell, then slowly turns to go.
A slight stirring movement catches his eye,
and a familiar voice weakly calls out his name.
It's a friend since childhood who's wounded and about to die.

The man leans over him and answers him with his name.
Their eyes meet for only a moment in time,
and the man holds his hand and speaks to him once more.
His friend slips away, and the man begins to climb
the steep, grassy slope of the hill.
He climbs to the top, where the land meets the sky.
In his hand is his friend's fine sword he used in the fight.
And he says farewell to his friend and raises it high.
He plunges it deep in the earth and grass with a sigh.
And it remains there still, as it did that night.
Many centuries have now past.
But the sword still shines and glimmers,
and the men are in a history that will last
as long as the sea by the hill still shimmers.
Do you see them? I still do.

Loraine R. Sparks

September 11

September 11, 2001, was the worst day
3,000 Americans killed
Osama bin Laden is a bad man
USA is fighting a war on terror
Some of my heroes are fighting for my freedom
Go USA
Think about the people who were killed on 9/11
If your team loses it's not as bad as what happened on 9/11/01

Ned Corkery

My favorite number is seventeen and my favorite color is red. Go USA. I wrote about 9/11 because it was the worst day ever. It's something you should talk about.

Reality

Three steps back and you're in the past;
Forget what is yet to come, for that I have won.
I call your name to be in sweet tame,
To breathe and be within your game.
I fell to what I felt without a second tame,
Giving reality such a sweet name.

Dounya Zeineddine

Slave

The term slave comes to mind as I sit in my home
The walls are closing in on me, can't breathe, unable to hold my own

The children want to do as they please; the husband shouts out his
    demand
Slaving in the 21st century, my heart sinking with every command

They refuse to work together surrounded by confusion
My head is bouncing to and fro, my brain racing for a single solution

I try to release the pain—the mounting suppression
I work harder, it's not enough, I'm falling deeper into depression

My eyes full of sadness, past year full of sorrow
Shattered hopes, I don't look forward to tomorrow

Eyes that have become tearless through the years of sorrow
Frustration, despair, humiliation, bitterness, fatigue
A slave, that I am

Searching for an answer to find a way out
From the world which has enslaved me all about
My spirit lost, a soul full of plea
The madness unbearable
What I wouldn't give for an ounce of serenity

Danielle T. Johnson

Crows

Waking up
with dreams of flight
underneath the full moonlight
look around the room
there is nothing different
in sight.

As I run down the stairs there is only the sound of silence in the air
I start my daily routines walking my dog through the cool morning
breeze
Walking along the countryside roads
Gravel loose underneath my feet
As I admire the rain of the fire like leaves

We watch the crows on top of the trees
Sitting in rows along the power lines
There seem to be more
Hundreds, no thousands, were flying above in the air

If I could, I wouldn't stop to stare
Not even a second nor a minute to spare
As we walked faster and further across the street
I can still hear them cawing in a rhythmic beat
I can't feel my feet, so I stop in frustration.
In the corner of my eye billions of crows circling high above
I stand there mesmerized looking to the crow-blackened sky
It came down around me everywhere
I closed my eyes and made a call in despair
But the next thing I knew I was in the air
The cawing got louder and the wind blew harder
A tingling sensation all around my whole body

I opened my eyes, I'm on the ground
There is nothing to be found
Not a single bird in the air
So I hop to a puddle and what do I see?
A crow staring right back at me

Omar Panjwani

You and Me

What's upside down to me
is right side up for you.
There's so much I can't see
and so much you can do.
Even when I'm spinning,
reeling 'round and 'round,
God I know You're winning,
You're my solid ground.

Carla De Vos

I am a very young contestant and I am honored to be a semi-finalist. I write many different kinds of poems. I like to write silly poetry, poems about the seasons, angry poems, sad poems, happy poems, etc. Writing is a job that I hope to have when I'm older. I love the arts as in drawing, dancing, and writing. I am ten years old.

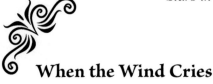

When the Wind Cries

The wind screams, but I can't hear it.
All I can pick up
Is the sound of my blood falling from my wrist and crashing to the
floor.
It shatters into a million tiny beads.
What have I done?
What has my life become?
I hear a knock on the door.
I make no attempt to answer it.
Suddenly I hear a whisper
So faint it's hardly audible over the dripping of my blood.
As a pool of beautiful scarlet forms beside me,
The whisper grows louder.
"Who is that?" I cry,
Scared for what's left of my life.
The whisper seems to be talking me down;
"Why not just end your life completely?
Don't suffer my child,"
It taunts me.
I feel this presence pulling me deeper into the darkness.
"Stay with me forever."
I hear a crash and realize someone is now with me,
Holding me in their arms.
I look into the beautiful blue eyes of my love.
What have I done?
I hear a scream saying no!
I close my eyes and start to shake.
What's happening?
Wind fills my room,
Tearing pictures off the walls.
The screaming air engulfs my body and carries me away,

Ripping me from the arms of my love.
The wind screams and takes me away.
I am gone forever because the wind whispered to me, and I did not listen.

Brii Au

Help

He's always kept his feelings inside.
Never wants anyone to see him cry.
Feels like his whole worlds crashing down. Defeat.
He knows he has been beat.

Help me get out of here.
Help me get rid of my fears.
Help, I'm screaming your name,
Hoping that you're doing the same.
I know I can't help myself, but with you, I'm someone else.
Everyone knows I've wept, so this is my cry for help.

She sits there in the second bathroom stall,
Eating alone…she sits there in a ball,
Crying her eyes out, wanting to be accepted.
All the scars, everything she's done, always to herself, she has kept it.

They sit together at lunch,
Dressed in all black. And he gets punched.
"Black eye to match your clothes," he says.
That night was the night Alan had ended the rest of his days.

Help me get out of here.
Help me get rid of my fears.
Help, I'm screaming your name,
Hoping that you're doing the same.
I know I can't help myself, but with you, I'm someone else.
Everyone knows I've wept, so this is my cry for help.

Every day, someone ends their life,
With that rope or taking their life,
All because people are judgemental idiots.

I picked up that suicide note,
Apologies to everyone he's hurt.
Tell my parents I love them so.
I'm sorry, but I really have to go.

I need help...

Tatyanna Blaylock

He Took the Road Less Traveled

He took the road less traveled, fulfilled his destiny
He gave his all his heart and soul and left a legacy
A life that mattered to us all, full of grace purpose and love
Such unselfish dedication his family did he give
We watched him with gratitude and pride
No disdain could we impart
Loving thoughts, precious memories we'll treasure for all time
There was no guile no malice, God's word he lived and loved
Words did not come easily, but his love was felt and known
We knew the words unspoken were no less felt or shown
His memory, his purpose we'll treasure for all time
Our dad, God's gift, his love we will enshrine
Thanks, Dad, for all the lessons, the precious gift you gave
It's felt and treasured in our hearts, its imprint forever made
Let's honor his example, can we do any less than he
Pure motives, dedication, we honor your memory
We'll love you, Dad, and remember with heartfelt sincerity
Your purpose and message sacrifice and devotion will live on through
    eternity

Linda Hart

This poem has a special meaning to me that is too personal to share. I would just like to say it was divinely inspired. In fact, I believe it is God's very words. This came to me at a time when I was in dire need of God's guidance.

Cyber Bullying

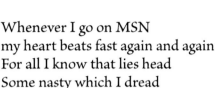

Whenever I go on MSN
my heart beats fast again and again
For all I know that lies head
Some nasty which I dread

Jade, you're this, Jade, you're that
Or even Jade, you're an ugly rat!
Oh leave, Jade, for Heaven's sake

She knows she's made a terrible mistake
For passing along her MSN
just scribbling it down with her fancy pen

I didn't think, I didn't care
And now I think it's just not fair
Who's doing this to me? Who's tearing me apart?
Who thinks they're so smart?

I know I have done something wrong
It doesn't mean you should say things that are way too strong
you destroyed my cheerful day and my sleepy nights
putting my name on comments that wear terrible for my eyes
When I walk into school
People point at me, they treat me like a fool

When I gave my email away it took my dignity and flew away
I wish I had a time machine
Way back before I wore the school green
I'll erase it from history

Now that this poem has come to an end
I'd like to say thank you for reading, my friend

Jade Marie Williamson

*My poem was inspired by my life. I have experienced some bullying about
my weight. I expressed the way I feel through poetry. I was not expect-
ing to be a semi-finalist. I'm very surprised and happy at the
same time.*

Autumn Remembers

I lay on the couch listening to the silent leaves fall outside the window
The falling leaves are whispering to me for all the times I avoided my
husband
For all the excuses I made not to be with him
For all the eye contact I consciously looked away from
The leaves are silently speaking to me to get up
But the smell of pumpkin seeds demands me to stay

I lie on the couch taking in the aroma of pumpkin seeds baking in the
oven
The scent of pumpkin seeds is mocking me for all the times I missed
dinner
For all the times I broke our wedding vows
For all the times I didn't say "I love you"
The pumpkin seeds are persuading me to get up
But his soft snoring is asking me to stay

I lie on the couch rubbing my socks against his, as he snores
His snores are yelling at me for all the times I burnt dinner
For all the times I slacked on the laundry
For all the times I neglected the vacuuming and the dusting
His snores scream at me to get up
But the warm fire beckons me to stay

I lie on the couch watching the fire dance
The fire crackles at me for all the times I stayed late at work
For all the times I cried on the phone
For all the times I made promises to God
The fire pops at me to get up
But the breath of the puppy on my arm summons me to stay

I lie on the couch gazing at the puppy inhale and exhale
The puppy's sweet breath is teasing me for all the times I tried to have a
    child
For all the times the doctors told us about impossibilities
For all the times I believed in hope, dreams, and miracles
The puppy's breath is taunting me to give up
Why does autumn have to remember?

Erika Nelson

Control

There are things in life you can control things you can't control
One thing you can control is how much control you give the things you can't control
Be the boss of your soul. Your heart works there
Never quit...pain doesn't write checks
But it does give stamps, sending your mind places it never wanted to be
Getting lost, no return address
Then where do you go from there?
Broke...in, in ways indescribable
Now, homeless and hungry
You're starving...gotta eat
Need nourishment (love), motivation (trust), commitment (job)
Then you could get paid (happiness)
No longer will you have a broken home
Everything falls back into place
Grasping life, your life, your love, yourself...self-control
There are things in life you can control and things you can't control
One thing you can control is how much control you give the things you can't control

Priscilla "Prii" Rosado

I Am Ready for Love

I am ready for love—no ifs ands or buts
The bruises, scrapes and the cuts
That come along with opening yourself to someone else
And welcoming them to discover the essence of you
I'm ready for a love so true
So strong
A love that defeats all
A love that will stand the test of time
I'm ready to make someone all mine
I want what one cannot define
Something that crosses all boundaries, all stereotypes
A feeling that will keep me warm at night
I am ready for a love that is oh so right that it can't be wrong
And if it is I've already gone too far
I'm in too deep
I'm ready for love to sweep me off my feet
I wanna go to a place where everything seems steep,
But it's simple when it comes to you and me
And you understand without me having to say
I am ready for a love that surpasses all words
I am ready for a love that cannot be heard
I am ready to give
I am ready for love
I am ready to live

Ahaviyah Pendleton

God is truly my love, which is what Ahaviyah means. I am twenty-four years old and I've been writing or creating before I realized that that is what I was doing. I love to write; it is my passion and what I fully believe God put me on this earth to do. I write for the everyday people what I see and feel, and I hope that they get a peek inside of me.

Free Me from This World

From this place I wish to be my own,
Run away from all that I know.
Exhaust from the passing cars fills my lungs,
Exasperated from my journey, there is no time for rest.

My thoughts fill my head, as I walk,
Exactly as I dreamed it would be.

Free from it all, nothing bonds me.
Rage that once filled my veins no longer exists.
One day at a time, thankful for every breath,
My belongings rest on my back.

They say you need school to have a future.
Hell, how would they know?
Imagining only the life they could've had
Shows me that I must prove them wrong.

Why do something that doesn't make me happy?
Oh, how I pity the future generations.
Reality?
Let us find true happiness and satisfaction without the world.
Dreamer is what they think of me.

Benjamin Reisinger

Who I Am: Somebody

Judge me not for who I am.
Judge me for being me.
I am who I am: somebody
I am proud to be that person I became,
I've come a long way, I have no time to play.
Now my faith and life have shown me the way,
who I am: somebody.

Lisa Effit Kepney

The Wind Blows

The wind blows through my hair—takes me back to a time long ago.
I can't believe that this child I see is me.
I long to feel as that child did—full of life and wonder.
The wind blows through my hair now as then,
but there is a different feel, a different sound to it.
Could I or should I have lived differently?
Is my life the sum of all my memories, all my actions or more?
The wind blows through my hair as the days of my life pass away.
Existence is changes in the physical and the wind is eternal.
Let the wind blow through my hair. I am fading away.

Karen J. Gilliam

I have written poetry to explore who I am and reflect back to who I was. I ask all the questions that most people do. We all wonder who we are and why we are. The poems expose the thoughts and feelings that frequently turn spiritual. We are all pilgrims in life and we must find our own way. Poetry is inner beauty.

Moonman

The Moonman looks down upon me
His whimsical hands wrap everything that is my world
Their fingers caress my skin so softly
As he pulls my body like the waves
In my very own bliss, I surround myself with Moonman
Holding onto him, knowing he won't let me go
The Moonman has me trapped in his rays
And I know I belong there
He says he will never leave me alone
And as the sun rises, my Moonman must set

Elizabeth Rein

Seven Years

Defied odds so uneven not a soul gave us a chance,
We left aimless and scared I packed all the wrong pants!
Excited for change we travel hand in hand.
Together was four and between us not one plan.
Packed helplessly into one leaky minivan,
I asked for an angel and was given much more.
Closed curtains slammed windows but keeps opening doors.
This is just the beginning, no idea what's in store.
For the next twenty years then the last eighty-four.
Don't think it could happen we have heard this same song.
As all those before who cried, they won't last long!
Together we grow stronger an unbreakable bond.
(pause)
Seven years of your life you dedicated to me.
No gift could express what this day means, you'll see
When we look back together at all the great memories!

Ian McRyhew

Untitled

Hail! Hail! The gods are here
Arriving on majestic vessels
Waves split before the dragon's head
One by one awakening from their beds
Rustling cloth and glimmering mail
Winds from the north filling the sail
Stomp of leather boots pounding the sand
Many an enemy felled by the sword in my hand
Crimson liquid drenching the cloth of the one God
Bejeweled idols taken as compensation for the loss of their brethren
Fear not! For a great hall awaits our fallen brothers!
As the sun sets what once was thirty is now twenty-four
Six women who would know the touch of a man no more
Countless children who shall not know a father's love anymore
So raise a horn in their honor and lament
Hail! Hail! May they be merry in the great hall above!

Nathen Christian

Originality

I pursue
The next part of my dream

On a narrow, winding road
I trip over other people
as I search
For the life that I've lost

I wish that you'll understand me

Stop making that sad face
Like you've been sacrificed
There aren't tears at the end of sins

The labyrinth of emotions, where I can't see the exit,
Tries to deviate my path

Isn't life still too long
For erasing these thoughts?

It seems like I've forgotten
In the middle of the night

I can fulfill myself
I quietly closed my eyes
I can even see
I'm alive

Robert Nolin

We'll Fly

I came to the land of opportunities,
Found out they couldn't see my credibilities.
I stepped up to the plate
Knowing it's not too late,
Being the best that I can be,
Hoping one day I'll be free.

Little money,
Big dream,
Ready to ride the fast stream,
The system will be broken;
We'll throw it right at them.
Heated blood runs through my veins
Remembering excruciating pains.

Going through customs,
Eyes all around me,
All hands on me,
Stripping through my dignity,

Who am I?
I'm Persian,
African,
Asian,
Afghan,
Colombian,
And Caucasian.

Barriers we'll walk by
With a smile on our faces
No matter what our race is
And fly.

Jojo Logo

Bound Loose

Craving for justice, an outcry
That has been kept low
Rises to be heard by us all
For others to know

Feeling burdened and beyond despair
We cling to our hopes
That others have tied down
With binding tight ropes

Loosened, we are freed from this strife
Cast on us by the foe
Who enforced a slavery life
Bringing us so much woe

Liberty is granted at last
We now have a true voice
In sharing with others our past
Freely, given the choice

Princess Brown

Jagged

Beautiful mess
He doesn't inspire me to write
There are no five page sonnets expressing my love for him
The truth is, there are no words
They are stuck somewhere
It's just he and I and space and silence, and it's okay
It's not perfect or comfortable
There is no confusion, the borders are clear, the lines is drawn in the
     sand
He does not love me; I am aware of that, but still
He is a real moment, not one I had to create on paper
He just is who he is
A beautiful mess of contradictions and confusion
Pain and loss
He needs no poetic words, his entire existence is poetic
The realist who brings all dreamers down to Earth
Cold and warm at the same time and just as lost and confused as I am
He is not perfect, but he is amazingly broken into jagged pieces that
don't fit together
I try to put them together and they cut my hands
A beautiful mess he is

Niove Rodriguez

Push Me, Pull Me

I pass you on the street and you give me that look, you pull me in, baby set the hook. You tell me that you need me but I know it's a lie, how many times have you made me cry?

Hey don't you know it ain't cool, the way you push me, pull me, baby, you fool me

Call me up, tell me to rush over, take me in your arms like a long lost lover. When the morning comes you make it clear you want my ass up out of here

Hey! Don't you know it ain't cool, the way you push me, pull me, baby, you fool me

I'm done with you ain't playing no more, don't text me, tweet me Facebook Poke me! I can't take the pain of your little game

Hey! Don't you know it ain't cool, the way you push me, pull me, baby, you fool me!

Hey! Baby, when you gonna call me?

Michael Hair

Purge

Remember when life didn't hurt,
when first assumption would be,
obviously...
the red is only spilt ketchup?

Don't be quite so strange.
Sad people are nearly thirteen.
You've grown out of the pain...
You've become accustomed to this world of gain.
It's acceptable..and smart!
Skinny is meant for extreme art.

Gag me twice and hear it pour.
I want to fail...if this number's my score.
Drop to the bottom as you fall to the floor,
I've finally come to see what my fingers are for.

Dawn Schwantke

From the Outside In

In her eyes
There is a sadness
And in her air
A manner of being
In her heart there is a whole
One with a meaning
Of never knowing
A sense of home
In her soul
A longing
To give back
In her mind
There is a stream
Of immortal thoughts
And a constancy of befalling dreams
In her touch
A sensation
A courage and a power
A fear and a frustration
In her words
Experience and meaning
Beyond her share
Of wounds from endless burning
But in her
Lies a light
One that has never gone out and never will
A hope
Held for more than just herself
Larger than the length
Or depth of any ocean

A truth
That will never lie
And a will
That never stands down

Alandra Nicole Moreira

We all lose ourselves at some point, but there are things within us that we can make sure that we can always find ourselves again. These things make our manner of being. I wrote this poem about me when I was confused about where I was, am, and wanted to be. I wrote it to remind myself that no matter how many times I lose myself, fail, succeed, or change, these things about me will remain constant; for what is cannot not be, and that is what a manner of being is.

Clouds of Grey

Mother Earth,
once filled with life,
her green children once grew tall
reaching for the sky.
Her pets once roamed
the land, sea, and air.
Those days are now gone.
Mother Earth's green children
are now being cut down in their prime
only to find titans of steel
taking their place.
Her pets are dying,
their homes disappearing,
destroyed to make room for poisonous giants
that spit out clouds of grey.
Why is this happening?
Mother Earth is dying.
Why would we do this to her?

Jonathan Pittman

Selena Gomez

Sweet, a world changer
Kind to many less
She is so open-hearted
These are some of the many words to describe Selena Gomez
With much more a great friend, lucky and blessed
Nevertheless
She is strong, brave, and kind
Worth much more than a dime!
Talented and great!
This super star has much more on her plate
Than the hair, eyes and all the cries, like most famous people
But true honest and always down-to-earth
Like the people she cares about the most
Selena, it's you who has inspired me as I wish to do for you

Destiny Lockhart

We Still Want You—Verse 1

Av, this song is like my
Eyes are speaking to you clearly through
The feelings that I deal with
And all the tears that fell for you
The pain's insane yet lovers' rain
It comforts as we feel our strain
We will retain a sweetness sayin'
It won't remain our dying shame
Our master's at our mercy
And he knows it could be worse see
But we can't stop all our knowing
While he cries he thinks, "This hurts me"
Know we're loving your perspective while your
Love is all reflective
And through all the time he's hurt
Our owners never felt neglected

Chris Henderson

Silent Sorrow

I know you're gone and that's a fact,
But my mind won't let me believe that
I'm sorry for my tears of pain and silent sorrow
I just cant believe I won't see you tomorrow
I know you're gone and that's a fact
But I will never believe that

Kacandra Bogan

Hello my name is Kacandra Bogan. I am fifteen years old. I wrote this poem and many others. This one is my favorite, though, because I wrote it when my great-grandfather died. I didn't know him very well. To be honest, I only met him once or twice, but when he died, it had a huge impact on my life mentally. It's crazy how people you barely know have major effects in your life.

All the Way Through It

In the dead of night came a dark and cold shadow
lurking upon our family, pulling and tugging away
at your life. Trying its very hardest to take you away
from us not knowing just how strong your little
heart really was. For a short time as death wrapped its
cold arms around you pulling and dragging you
further from us thinking it finally had you in its
grasp for the taking, God stepped in and surrounded
you with all His love and mercy bringing you back to
the life you were not supposed to be leaving yet. Who
would have ever guessed that of us all, you the smallest
would be pushed past the breaking point and yet still
come back swinging, pushing, and fighting for your life
All the way through it!

Alexandra Ortiz

When I wrote this poem I was going through a very hard time; I almost lost my older sister. But by the grace of God she was saved. I feel like poetry has always had a huge impact in my life, it has always been my way of letting out everything and expressing what I need to say even without saying a word.

Easter Blessings

Easter blessings with a whispering voice from God above
He told me to search for your sweet love
And with no hesitation I did just as I was told
As days and months went slowly by
You began to show a side of you that put my heart and soul in disbelief
That what I had prayed for had somewhere gone wrong
Each morning I awake holding onto the blessings that were when we
    first began
Now and then I still sing God's grace and see our love shine
In the dark of night that once was an Easter blessing in my soul

Mary Rhodes

Rest His Soul

Vietnam was an era, a decade of time that would weld in us concern.
We would leave our homes and fly to a place where we had to learn.

Their people didn't like us much. With guns they'd shoot to kill.
The bullets would rip through our flesh, then our blood would spill.

The phone would ring. His mother would answer. Then her eyes
would tear.
His father would sit with shaking hands. He knew of all the fear.

Their son has died with honor we're told, as they fall in slumber.
Another man, another life, he won't be just a number.

Bitter thoughts confuse the heart. The memories don't go away.
His gentle touch, with spoken words, it's going to be okay.

All gave some and some gave all, the patch my brothers wear.
We ride for freedom and tell the world we will always care.

The old man cried, his thoughts would tear the memories from his
heart.
A bullet had taken his brother's life. Sixty years they've been apart.

And now I look into his eyes, they're wet with grief, it's sad.
He closed his eyes to rest his soul—
This old man was my dad.

Gerald Robinson

*I was born on September 24, 1951, and sixty years went by in a blink. To know
me is to learn of my past. There is much wisdom gained in our walk through life.
When we favor a word so the reader can taste the sweet or bitter moments that
emotionally attract the writer, we can then feel the success as a poet. This poem
was written for my dad. He lost his only brother in the Korean conflict. What a
shame to spend this life with torment and grief. We are only passing
through, love deep and live complete.*

Take the Time

I stand stoically and with solemnity,
Perplexed at the alluring prairie which calls out to me so silently with
    its resounding resources,
Showcasing its glorious grace, strong with senses.

I stare so boldly at the beautiful, barren
Desert, dawdling dreamily, unseen by so many
As they hurry on their way. Time is the traveler's master; and they
    cannot waste it on a prairie.

I see new sagebrush as it slowly
Surges on with strength, emerald grasses for grazing goats.
The few trees teased by the breeze with arms raised in peace to the
    heavens.

I feel the soft wind caress my being
Trying to peek under my skirt and then run away like a schoolboy.
The dust devils spray sand in circles;
It burns my face like a million shards of crystal.

I hear wings of vultures vying for
Scraps of something, screeching at all others
To stay away from the prize that is theirs.
Songbirds' sublime tunes make me close my eyes for now.

Ilamae Stucki

'Twas the Day I Saw You

'Twas a day I won't forget
And a day I won't regret
As I sat there on the couch
And started to watch and slouch

Don't know what it is in you
Think I did fall for you too
With those oh so boyish grins
Even the night could not dim

I don't care about the bod
But man, yours isn't that bad!
And add to your matching wit
All the girls can't help but writhe

'Twas the day I first saw you
The day I got into you
Encino opened the door
And I hoped to see you more

My favorite though is still Rick
Along with Evelyn, you click
Though *The Mummy* has been gone
The legend stays to carry on

I'd be honest I'm at a lost
Not sure why I joined this cause
One thing, though I'm sure about
Is I'm proud to join this bout

So, 'twas the day I saw you
That one day I had no clue
My heart you stole, it's true
'Cause of you I won't be blue

Aileen Mendoza

I am from the lovely islands of the Philippines. I love to write! I write when I'm sad, I write when I am happy. I write about the weather and the clouds. I write about everything I can think of. I started writing in my diary then I started writing poetry for my family and friends. It was my essay "The Reunion" that was published in a local magazine that made me realize that I could write. And I hope to write more.

Big Blue Eyes

You,
With the big blue eyes,
Shinning brightly,
Brighter than the skies,
Why won't you choose me?
Choose me as your own?
I don't wanna stand here,
Stand here on my own.

With your big blue eyes,
Uh oh,
With your dark brown hair,
Uh oh
You make me wanna stare
At you
All day long.

Alannah Jones

Katy Your Perfect

Katy Perry
Perfect name for a perfect person.
No two ways I try to see her are enough.

Colour,
Style,
Spunk.

Katy always brings these three things to everything she does.
She connects with her fans
and helps us through all the difficult times we face.

To do such a thing you need a special kind of perfectness.

And Katy,
You are the only has who will ever have it!

Zoe Pereira

Twenty-Two Years of a Colourful Rainbow

Crouched in the corner crying
The weight of the world falling on you like a rainbow
Colouring your life with misery and regret
Is there anything you can do to forget?
Knees in your chest feeling the rhythm of your heart
Fingers intertwined with your hair, grasping at your head
These thoughts will not leave, these thoughts will not let down
The constancy of replaying your life, twenty-two years in twenty-two
　　seconds
Replayed for twenty-two hours
Two hours of silent sleep, two hours of peace
Two hours of nothing that feels like twenty-two minutes
That feel like twenty-two seconds
That feels like nothing compared to this bright rainbow that hangs over
your head Dropping all the colours of a broken heart and a torn spirit
Every colour of depression, every colour that every eye on every human
　　has seen
Casting shadows so bright that you're clear as a sun in a blue sky
As clear as a rainbow after a thunderstorm
As clear as the tears in your eyes that overflow onto your face
Leaving traces of released hurt for the world to understand
That for the past twenty-two years you haven't seen the beauty of the
　　colourful rainbow But the pain the rainbow shines.

Norma Wiebe

*My name is Norma Wiebe. This year I will be twenty-four years old, and I have
had a problem with depression for the majority of my life. This poem is about me,
twenty-two years of a colorful rainbow describes the moods everybody feels in life
but dwells more on the negative. The negative always seems to impact lives first.
Writing has always been my outlet, and this poem has helped me to release some
　of the negative I keep inside.*

Tree Models

In Winter
you are such a sight
in your covering
of white

Then comes Spring
and what a thing
to watch you preen
your shades of green

In summer
you seem to slumber
as you give shade
and under your boughs, all life parade.

What a show in the fall
as you heed the North wind's call
colours of such shades and hues
prepare us well, for winter's blues.

Frances Wilson

Time Somebody Told Me

Time somebody told me
that everything will be okay
that the sun will set and
the moon will rise every day

Time somebody told me
that life will move on
and that I am not alone
that the day will come
when I see that stone

Time somebody told me
that the day will come
where we can all rest

Time somebody told me
that life comes to an
end whether we like it or not
We will all see that day no matter what

Time somebody told me
all I need to hear
Where are you now
when I need you most?

Jassmine Taylor

Love

You said it so simply,
like it was the only thing you could think of.
Those three little words that escaped your lips.
But you had other intentions.
I love you.
You threw the line like a fisher throwing his bait.
You reeled me in with those words.
And I was caught up in your game.
But now my eyes are open,
under the water I can see your line.
I swim right past it.
You're no longer mine.

Stephanie J. Fernandez

Those Are the Days

Those are the days
I will never forget,
The days I want back,
But I will never get,
The days you and me
Ran and fell on the grass,
The days it seemed
Happiness would never pass,
The times we kicked dirt
Until we couldn't see,
Because those were the days
We were so carefree.
Those were the days
We were inseparable
Because those were the days
We were unbreakable.
The days we played
Until the sun went down,
The days we weren't allowed
To go downtown,
The times we stayed up
Until just after dawn
Because they were the last days
Before summer was gone,
The days we felt
Scared and alone,
But when we were together,
We didn't want to go home.
The days I want back,
But I will never get—
Those are the days
I will never forget.

Bobbie Proctor

Poetry plays a fairly big role in my life. I find it inspirational and relaxing. This poem was inspired by my childhood memories of me and my best friend. I spent most of my time with him and neither of us really spent too much of our time with others. These are memories that mean a lot to me and I will always cherish them. My poem is about how we will always remember these times and hold them dear, but we will never be able to relive them under any circumstances.

The Human Condition

She hums quietly to herself.
The words escape her.
But the melody remains,
Louder now
And louder still.
A stranger on the street
Murmurs lyrics as he passes her by.
"That's it!" she cries.
"I know." he replies.
She turns to him.
He has already faded away.
She stares at a sea of expressionless faces.

She sings quietly to herself.
"That's it." Some faceless passerby murmurs.
She's already gone.

Alexis Vienneau

I am twenty-one years old and have been living with anxiety disorder since the age of fourteen. The constant and unexplainable fear led to feelings of depression and isolation from people and the world in general. I turned to poetry as a way to express my feelings and perception of life. "The Human Condition" was written during a time when I felt very out of touch with the world and the people inhabiting it. It echoes my feelings of being part of an anonymous society that doesn't pay close enough attention to its surroundings. However, this life is filled with many encounters and even the most fleeting can have a large impact.

This Is My Life

Confused is what I am,
Because You chose mine out of all the other plans.
You picked me up, with no intention of setting me down,
It's funny how we're always walking hand in hand.
I know You would never let me drown,
But I seem to just keep swimming down.

Down, down, into the tunnel of sin,
But You still always ask if I can let You in.

I open the door and we share many happy moments,
But then he creeps in too,
It's him, my opponent.
He brings back those terrible memories of sinful desires that I
    think I can't resist,
So the righteous man walks out with tears on his lids.

I have a periodic moment of joy,
Before my opponent comes again to collect my due.
They say whatever he giveth,
he taketh away from you.

So here I am, all broken and battered,
There's a knock on the door,
Hmmm, so I still flatter?
I open the door and to my surprise,
the righteous man is standing with desire in his eyes.
With no doubt, I bring him in.

Now, my life is whole again.

Ruth James

*This poem came to me when someone challenged me to write a poem in about
thirty minutes or less (which I didn't exactly accomplish). It caused me to think
of the situation I was in at the moment, and I decided to put it on paper. My
poems are usually about what's going on in my life or a close friend's, and a
lot of the times I like to write about God because it is the best way to
let my emotions out on how I feel about Him on the inside.*

There's a Girl in My Mirror

There's a girl in my mirror crying tonight
And there's nothing I can say to make her feel alright
She has been beaten and bullied by kids that don't know what's right
But still she manages to smile when she's filled with fright

There's a girl in my mirror who picks up a knife
She was ready to take her own life
Blood flows down her arm like rain
She said that she was going though pain
But then I realized it was just a reflection
Of the child in me that suffered from rejection
It reflected not only the outer but the inner me
And all the scars we couldn't see

There's a girl in my mirror who wanted to change her life
So she decided to throw away the knife
The kids at school made fun of her still
But sometimes scars you can't see are the hardest to heal
I don't want to keep being the girl that keeps crying about the same
    things
I want to be the girl that was able to spread her wings
When something goes wrong I won't run to death
So if you're waiting don't hold your breath

Keyahna "Keya" Curry

Lost Souls

What I see is what holds me back
I know in this area I lack.
What I know is how to overcome
Even though it's hard to some.
What I hear are the voices
Screaming out above the noises.
What I smell is the decay
Of all that death has eaten away.
What I touch is a child's tears
Grown up in too short of years.
What I taste is the burnt ashes of a fire
Set ablaze with hate as one's desire.
Passion filled
Passion killed.
A ticking time bomb waiting to explode
Their life has led them to implode.
No one can help them finish the story untold
Once filled with treasures of gold.
Now in this time
We bring to mind
All the lost who have taken their lives as tolls
Never to finish their dreams and goals.
They fade into the background
Bent till they back down.

Cheyenne Garrett

My poem's origin came from a conversation with my best friend I had a few years back. It was about suicide and what drives a person to end it all. Truth be told, I still haven't found a solid answer. To me, poetry is a way to leave my mark on the world. I don't want to fade into oblivion and I want future generations to look at me and say, "I want to be like her, if she can do it then so can I." I want to be a positive role model. I want to show teenagers that dreams can come true. God bless you.

Wide Awake, but in the Dark

The sky was grey and I must say,
"It truly was a dreary day."
I shut the window and the door,
and the sky rained more and more.
I lay down in my lumpy bed,
pulled my covers up over my head.
My body trembled and my bed shook.
I was too scared to take a look.
I would not open up the door.
No more rain. No more. No more.
So there I lay deep in my bed—
too scared to move, too filled with dread.
I knew the sun was far away,
that I would not see light that day.
The darkness seeped into my thoughts,
as it unlocked my scary vaults.
It opened scars, uncovered pain.
It unleashed memories tucked away.
This blackness surely was the end.
A bird's-eye view would be my friend.
But hoping for a cloudy scene
was nothing but a hopeless dream.
So there I lay, still wide awake,
this darkness more than I could take.
And just when I could hardly breathe,
a ray of light shone through my sheets.
I pushed them back, rose from my bed,
my coffin saved for when I'm dead.
I crossed the floor and opened the door.
The sun shone down, and it rained no more.
Happiness replaced my sorrow,
as I looked upon my bright tomorrow.
My eyes burned and then I cried.
My life was before me when I thought I had died.

Lauren French

Am I in the Mood for Food?

Cookies, cakes, brownies too
Everything's for me and you
I would love to eat it all
But I just got a special call
From the doctor saying that
I am getting really fat
It looks so delicious though
Will I eat it? I don't know
What I need to do is think
Should I even take a drink?
Well, I guess that I just might
Take a teensy eensy bite
But which one should I choose?
This is starting to make me fuse
Cherry, grape or pumpkin pie
Blue or yellow food dye
Feast or meal or a snack
I might have a heart attack
I guess I just won't eat at all
'Cause this order's just too tall!

Brenna Clarine

Who We Are

There is a girl who looks like me yet I do not know who she is
She looks like me
She moves as I do
She even sounds like me when she speaks
Her thoughts aren't as mine though
She loves crowds of people
but I prefer to be alone
She coasts through life without a care
but I carry the weight of the world
She sings blissful songs of hope, faith, and light
Yet I sing songs of woe and despair
When I inhale so does she
But she inhales life
I inhale sorrow
Who is she?
She is how the world sees me
I am the truth

JaLisa Adams

Lost Cries

Tears fall onto the lunar rose
During the chill of the night.
A wolf cries for the one that is lost them,
Who knows if they will ever be found.
The thunder of paws hit the ground like a crystal blue wave
Crashing against the vacant shore.
That shore is the same as this heart of mine,
Lost to those who search for my soul.

Michaela Ezell

Remember Me

Remember me when you see a smile so bright and cheery or
    quirky and funny,
when you hear a bird singing or crafting a nest,
when you see a car all bright,
shiny or rusted out—but a classic,
when you dance in the twilight or just sleep the day away.

Remember me when a dream comes true,
when you feel a caress on your face,
when you turn back, wondering if someone is watching you,
when you think no one else is watching over you,
remember me, for I will always be there for you.

Remember me when you feel the rain on your face,
reminding you to buy an umbrella—again,
when you feel the wind go through your hair, messing up the
    perfect do,
when you feel snow on your nose, oh so cold,
wanting someone to warm you,
when you feel the sand on your feet,
the water lapping at your toes, teasing you to come in.

Remember me when a dream comes true,
when you feel a caress on your face,
when you turn back wondering if someone is watching you,
when you think no one else is watching over you,
remember me for I will always be there for you.

Remember me when you plant a garden, mow the yard,
or go yard saling,
when you go swim in your new suit,on a picnic,
or row a canoe,
when you go apple picking, pumpkin plucking
or trampling through a corn maze,
when you trim the lights, carve the turkey or
exchange a kiss for a new year.

Elvira Scaff

Confused

How can you think of someone in the arms of someone else?
How can you just hang your feelings for them on a shelf?
How can something so wrong feel so right?
I never thought I'd do this, but then again I just might.
How can one heart feel so much strain?
I feel sad, I feel guilty, I feel mad and ashamed.
How can I do this? Go on in this way?
I know I have to tell him, but what do I say?
With one I feel happy, safe, and at home,
but with the other I can be myself, alive and unsewn.
I have to make a choice, I know I have to choose,
but what could I be missing, and what could I lose?
Which path do I take? Which road do I follow?
One could leave me fulfilled, and the other leave me hollow.
I care for one, but long for the other,
I can't take it anymore, I'm gonna run for cover.
But I can't, I can't run, can't hide from my fate.
I gotta face it, be strong, and make my mind up before it's too late.
So here I go. Wish me luck.
I've made my decision, and there's no turning back.
You only live once, and I wanna live it all.
I'm gonna take the road less traveled and let myself freefall.
Hope I'm making the right decision, you never know what life will
    throw,
but you have to go through hardships and let yourself grow.

Ashley Marcinew

I love to write! I've been writing poetry and short stories for as long as I can remember. I wrote my first love poem when I was only fourteen years old and I had no idea what love was, though I knew I wanted to be a part of it. I've always been a hopeless romantic. This poem is about a painful choice you have to make between two people you care about. I hope you enjoy reading my work as much as I enjoyed writing it.

To Garden Forever

The beauty of the world has two edges,
One of laughter, one of anguish.
Beauty is not in the face; beauty is a light in the heart.
Memories are a way of holding onto things you love
The things you are and the things you never want to lose
Memories locked in your mind stop you from living.
Missing someone isn't about how long it has been
Since you've seen them, or how long it's been since you've talked.
Missing them happens in that moment when you wish they were right
　　there.
Once heard a bird sing in the dark of December
Such a magical thing, so sweet to remember
December the time for reflection, home and comfort.
An old gardener never dies they just go to seed
Everything ends with flowers—
We come from the earth, we return to earth, and in between we
　　garden.

Abigail Hale

The Air of Love

You are the air I breathe, and I love you for it.
My first breath when I open my eyes, it is you.
Most people walk around and never mind you,
But I appreciate you and I love you,
And I appreciate your love for me, you give me life.
So why would I let you go?
So I made you my wife,
And together share our love with the world in the air.

Bryant R. Thorpe

Since I was a child, I have always written things and loved it. I've always found inspiration from the Bible and the beauty and elegance of a woman's body. I'm from Stem, NC. My home, my wife, inspires me now. I write with feeling and emotions of her. I put my heart and soul into all that I do, that makes me feel infinite on paper and in thought. I love my wife and she strengthens me in all that I need to do. God has blessed me and I thank Him for it.

Cowboy's Curse

He rides buckin' broncos.
He rides till sunset.
He rides till he's broke.
His eyes are wilder than his horse's.
His clothes are old as his ranch.
His hair is thick as his horse's mane.
His body moves with the rhythm of country song.
He is smooth like leather,
The natural life of a cowboy.

Naomi Zurbuchen

My Meadow

The beautiful flowers that blow in the meadow are slowly moving in colors of orange and yellow. The warmth of the sun and the coolness of the breeze makes me smile and run with ease.

I lay down on the steppe hillside and watch the birds as they fly by. While the bees interact pleasantly with the pollen, they buzz in my ear as they soar up to the heavens.

The meadow is my place of peace and grace, my heart is at rest while I lay in my wonderful place. The love of the site of the colors so bright makes me sigh with this beautiful life.

Kelly Sheeran

Actually I was helping my daughter do a homework assignment. We were rushing to get ready for school when I told her to get ready and I will put something together quickly. I turned out to be very quick and I guess we cheated a little bit, but I didn't want her to get a failing grade. When she submitted the poem she was told it was the best poem in the class. We laughed when she told me. So when I saw this contest on the internet I thought why not submit it? My husband and family think writing is something I should pursue. So why not give it a try and see what happens? I want to thank my husband Terence and my daughters Kayla and Amanda. I love you—Mom.

I Tried to Laugh Today

I tried to laugh today,
    But cried instead.
I tried to smile today,
    But ran the other way.
I tried to love today,
    But hated instead.
I tried to see you today,
    But you looked the other way.

I wanted to call you today,
    But went walking instead.
I wanted to hold you today,
    But wound up holding myself.
I wanted to cry today,
    But decided to pray instead.

I decided to not cry today.
    I laughed instead.
I decided to stop running today.
    I grounded myself for a change.
I decided to not need you so much today,
    I learned that I need myself more.
I tried to leave this place today,
    But found that I needed to live.

Thank you for loving me as you did,
    For leaving me as you did,
For helping me find myself again.
I decided to be strong today,
And that's just what I did.

Marjorie Banks

*I am a fifty-year-old wife, mother, and grandmother. I've been writing poetry since
I was twelve years old. My poems express my thoughts, feelings, dreams and fears.
I write from my heart and head. I am working on a book of poetry, current-
ly untitled and have been published in a book titled* From a Poetic
Point of View"

Once Upon the Blind

Once upon
a long time ago
deep in a dank,
dark cave,
the only things
that could be seen
were two eyes,
bright and shiny,
round and twinkling
like the stars,
stars placed deep
in a dark abyss
called a face,
the windows
to the soul, perhaps.
But not these eyes;
these eyes could not see,
for the dark was thick
and they blinked
alone.

Emily Holland

Porcelain

Rose-painted cheeks,
Porcelain painted skin,
We sit on our shelves, lovely and perfect.
But our hearts are cracked from what we endure.
Our pink lips are glued shut,
Not able to express our pain, our frustration.
Because, of course, we were molded to be perfect.
Socially, physically, mentally.
Dolls, let us stand up on our dusty shelves,
Let us raise our glass voices in defiance, let us speak the truth.
Our voices will shape the story of our trials,
How it doesn't matter how we are made,
How pretty our dresses are,
How many times we've been dropped, cracked, broken,
We are all beautiful. We are all important. We are all connected.
We shall join our plaster hands,
And seal each other's broken hearts with glue made of love,
Compassion, friendship.
Let us make our imperfections, perfection.
We are porcelain, we are beautiful,
We are one.

Maddy Lobsinger

If I Could

If I could, I would love you the rest of my life.
If I could, I would take a while, just to make you smile.
If I could, I would do you right, and always hold you tight.
If I could, I would make us a nest, and fill it with happiness.
If I could, I would take all of your fears, and turn them into happy
tears.
If I could I would make you feel safe, while I'm kissing your face.
If I could, I would stay by your side, and make you my wife.
If I could, you know I would, love you the rest of my life.

Jim Reed

As If You Knew

How can I make this more obvious?
What is there to say about the way we were together?
    You told me and I listened. I believe you and still do

Your words were perfect and made so much sense
How much can honor and honesty save?
Honestly

Felt you at my worst. Had you at your best
All you have to do is smile and I'll do all the rest
Can't seem to regret the time I've spent wrapped up in your words
Crystal clear, letting me know just where you stand

Adam F. Pokrasky

I've been writing since I was eleven years old, although I'd like to think I've gotten better since then. It is the only thing I've done consistently for such a long time. This poem is loosely inspired by another artist and taking their words to heart. Sometimes art can speak to you in such a way that it feels more like a real-life conversation than merely an expression and a subsequent interpretation, and my piece roughly touches on that. I continue to write as it's the only accurate record of my thoughts and my moods.

Any Man Can Be a Father

From crawling to my first steps
I fell down and you haven't given up yet
Hand out, arms open, as I look up and reach
I am lost for words I cannot speak
You gradually moved into
My heart
You built shelter there
From the start
When I am shivering
You hand me your jacket
When I am stuttering
You become my vocabulary
When I am blind
You are my bifocals that lead me to the light
Your love is unconditional
Your acceptance is impeccable
Your faith is relentless
And your strive has left those among us breathless
Sick and all
You refuse to crawl
You always find your stance
And play your role as a man
I can't no longer has meaning in our dictionary
We have re-written I can in our pictionary
My mother is my everything
Life without her
Is like a bird with no wings
I will never say I can't fly without her push
But I can say I will try even when it looks harder than it should
My father told me to never say I can't
But my daddy taught me to always say I can
So even though I am not your seed
Instead of telling me you showed me

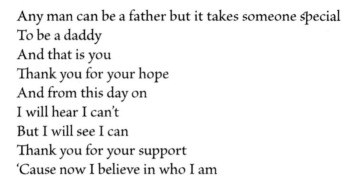

Any man can be a father but it takes someone special
To be a daddy
And that is you
Thank you for your hope
And from this day on
I will hear I can't
But I will see I can
Thank you for your support
'Cause now I believe in who I am

Ashleyrose Herald

Inner Child

I'm letting out my inner child,
the one who loved life on just this side of wild.
The one with dreams,
world of rainbow ponies, warm golden sun beams,
who danced in the barn with rake in hand
pretending there was music on a sandy tropical island.

The chickens cackled and raised their wings,
we had a fine time those chicks and I,
when the sun was due to rise, the rooster sings.
Time marches on, no more dances, the moon leaves only shadows.
My inner child rebelling, wanting out, middle age starts to show.
I say dance anyway, dream wherever you can,
let your inner child out,
even if it is to bang a pot with a ladle in the kitchen.

Julia Courey

As we get older, childhood memories become more and more cherished. I am inspired by living in the northwest with the mountains and ocean so close by. I love to write about collections of things, bringing in stories of objects, people who would not and cannot tell their own stories. Define poetry with love and let others' vulnerabilities evolve and diminish.

Keep Going

You are wonderful, beautiful,
perfect in your own ways.
Nothing can stop you,
nothing can break you
or your dreams.
So keep going, nothing can stop you.
So dream on, you made it far already.
No matter how wealthy, talented, popular,
everyone has at least one dream.
So keep going, no one can stop you.
So dream on, you progressed so much already.
Just keep goin'...
You must keep goin'...
I know you've been strong,
but I know you can get stronger.
Just like music,
you're energetic.
Just like music,
you're the main attraction.
C'mon, c'mon, c'mon.
You can do it,
So keep going, nothing can stop you.
So dream on, you made it far already.
You are wonderful, beautiful,
perfect in your own ways.
Nothing can stop you,
nothing can break you
or your dreams.
Yeah...c'mon!
No matter how wealthy, talented, popular,
everyone has at least one dream.
So keep going, nothing can stop you.
So dream on, you made it far already.

Just keep going.
You must keep going.
I know you've been strong,
but I know you can get stronger.
Just like music,
you're energetic.
Just like music,
you're the main attraction.
C'mon, c'mon, c'mon.
You can do it,
so keep going, nothing can stop you.
So dream on, you made it far already.
Yeah...c'mon!
Just keep going

Brianna Askey

loveless

you're beautiful but i don't want you anymore
you're priceless but you're not what i'm looking for
you're a distorted memory dying in my heart
you're mesmerizing but i'm craving for the dark

you're incomparable and i'm sinking in your ocean floor
you're flawless but your thirst for vanity is hard to ignore
you're uncorrupted and i'm just too vain
you're hopeless and i keep falling back to the same chains

you're perfect but perfection is controlled
you're filled with passion but all i feel is cold
I'm loveless and my heart can't take anymore.

Nadia Rahpaima

Born and raised in Dubai, ever since I was a kid I was always into poetry and writing. For me, poetry was an escape where I let my emotions run freely and let out on paper what I truly felt. It was cathartic for me. I recently moved to Canada to pursue filmmaking; it has always been my dream for people to see the world through my Ray Ban glasses. I consider myself an artsy person who appreciates all forms of art, which is why I like to convey it not only through writing but also painting, photography and filmmaking. People see me as a loud, obnoxious, optimistic person who's spontaneous, with a larger than life personality, but poetry brings out a more sadistic version of me that people never see. I wrote "Loveless" two years back when I was seventeen. It was a dark time in my life where I was going through something very personal and the only way I could deal with it was by writing my inner thoughts.

I Loved the Way

I loved the way we hugged and touched
I loved the way we laughed so much
I loved the way we used to fight
Then make love until the morning light
I loved the way we used to dance
And every single loving glance
I knew that I was your real, true love
 we were just like morning doves
I miss you so, my one true love
Please help guide me from the heavens above

The choices I've made since you've been gone
Haven't been the greatest ones
Please help me find my way
I still think of you every night and day
I know I should have moved on by now
Though I still cannot somehow
Especially when the best time in my life
Were with the one true love of my life

Sometimes things seem so dark and grey
Hopefully that will change someday
I know that your in a better place
Hopefully we'll meet again in another time, another place

Sonya Young

Keep It Simple

In our world of moving at the speed of, "Excuse me do you
need to find a restroom?" LOL

    Keep it simple...
Tell those you hold dear you love them, whether it be
your wife, husband, son or daughter, parents or siblings,
your close friends.

    Keep it simple...
Speak their language. For some I love you
means simply speaking the words.

    Keep it simple...
For others I love you means a look or smile
only translated by the one on the receiving end.

    Keep it simple...
Still others I love you means remembering 3 months ago
when she said, "That scarf would look amazing on me!"

    Keep it simple...
To you I love you means the perfectly planned day,
where every detail is carefully crafted and painstakingly
includes as much detail as one can take from memory and
incorporate in an afternoon or evening.

    Keep it simple...
They say love is blind. You're the last to see deception
but the first to see ambition, last to see rejection but first
to see potential, last to see their flaws but first to see your
perception of their perfection. (Only You) LOL!

    Keep it simple...
Years roll on like a roller coaster ride, 20s going up that first
steep hill, 30s you're thundering down by the seat of your pants,
in your 40s another hill to climb (So I am told). 50s you're cruising
along looking back and reminiscing.

    Keep it simple...

We need to be intimate (an unselfish desire to know another
created person in the overflow of all that is within) with one
another in our friendships love deeply, how much more towards
our significant other(s).

    Keep it simple...
Life, like traffic on the interstate or highway going east
and west at 100 miles an hour continues speeding on.

    Keep it simple...
We were created for so much more
than we perceive or can fathom…

Ian Georgescu

*In life we are faced with many challenges, and divorce is one that many of us deal
with. In all we do "speak life." Like a rose needs sunlight, so does your spouse.
Speak their love language, add water, and it will grow over time, don't diminish.
Water only comes from the one who created all things and loved us by dying for
us—one death, one time, and for all.*

Deep Within

My heart aches within from missing you,
My lips long for the feel of kissing you.
Right now all I need is to gently touch your skin,
To look into your eyes and see deep within,
Just one warm embrace,
Just to look upon your face,
Just one little touch,
From the one I love so much.
If I could gaze upon your smile
For just a little while,
To know that you miss me too,
As I'm thinking of you,
To hear the sound of you breathe,
Knowing you'll never leave,
To see you walk up to me,
Then embrace you tenderly,
To just be with the one who's sent my heart reeling
And brought about this downpour of emotion and feeling.
I sit here alone in my living room tonight
And pray that somehow this all turns out right.
I've never been one to do more taking than giving.
I'm not well off but I work hard for a living.
I've told you many thoughts that weren't borrowed or bought,
And in lifetime, who would have thought
That I have found someone who was just meant for me?
I can't explain the magic or why this should be,
But there is one thing that I know for certain,
That this just ain't over till one of us draws the final curtain.
For I've seen an angel and I want you to know,
If it's my choice to make, I'll never let you go.
Don't know what life holds, maybe there's no reason or rhyme

To think you may be mine in a matter of time.
And though I cannot touch you and we are now apart,
My love, you do dwell so deep within my heart.

Shayner Emmerson

A very lovely lady inspired me to write this poem. Thank you, Ms. Manda, for showing me I can be a better person. Though so many miles still separate us, my heart and soul belong to you!

A New Earth Leader

To Dalai Lama

Your presence enlightens
Your smile encourages
Your words have impact
Your energy is vibrant
You are nowhere and everywhere
You are the messenger of the New Earth
The time is now
You are a leader of kindness, wisdom, and compassion
A New Earth leader
Peace is in you
Peace is in me
Peace is in everyone

Mila Lansdowne

I am empowering people to use their talents and skills to unfold their full potential and to help others reach the same. I see the greatness in every person. When everyone lives in his or her purpose, prosperity and peace for all will be the outcome. A peaceful world for everyone will come as a result of our peaceful minds. I strive to lead by example.

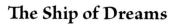

The Ship of Dreams

Burn, sizzle, catch a flame
Sit and relish in your undoubted shame.
I want to see you perish in such a torturous realm
Where heat, fire, and lava are at the helm
Of a ship so dead on a sea so black,
Fog so thick, you may never come back.
And whilst on the ship you'll meet a man,
Skin so blackened with ash that it looks like a tan.
Not a dollar to his name, no cash on hand,
Just a lifetime of tales, stories so grand.
Tales of bountiful riches, goblins,
And witches and fighting enemies so fatal
That your jaw will hit the floor, and you'll want to ignore
But also want to believe he was able.
Then he'll tell you one of his greatest stories
This one of which is especially gory.
He wipes debris from his beard and takes a drink of his forty.
"But he's a pirate," you think, "Did they have forties?"
You blink once, twice, three times, he's gone.
You run to the upper deck...and you're inside your home.
And just when you think you're alone,
You turn to the right and see a drone.
It's disguised as your mother, its arms made of butter,
And it's singing "Teenage Dream."
You go into a panic, run away very frantic,
And straight out your front door.
And you wouldn't believe what was up this world's sleeve
As you found yourself near your house no more.
You couldn't complain, the trees were candy cane
And just when you thought all was well
You took a step forth and there you fell

That's when it happened, you jumped upward and bumped your head
Then rubbed your new bruise...and whispered
"No more cake before bed."

Emily Barbour

I never thought by the age of seventeen that I'd be able to say that I am a published poet. Poetry has mainly been a hobby of mine since I was about ten years old. Sure, I was a kid who dreamed of reading my poetry in front of thousands and inspiring every single person. Although, I never thought I'd have the chance to do it. Poetry to me is an escape. When I have no one to talk to, I write. When I'm having a good day, bad day, boring time, anything—I just write. And, with this poem, I did just that. I wanted to create a world so vivid for the reader that it's almost as if they can see it when they close their eyes. I did this because I'm a writer who writes with her imagination more than her heart. If I can't see it, how do I know the reader will? Finally, I would just like to tell the world to not give up on something you love because of others. I've been made fun of for writing poetry, but it didn't stop me. If you believe in yourself, you can prove anything to the world. We all have something to prove because we are all unique and everyone matters.

Tell Me You Do

You say you love me, you say you do
but how do I know your words are true?

I stay up all night because of you
but that's because I don't know if you love me too

I think about all the great memories we had
but then I think of all the memories that are bad

I want to believe all the things you say
but when I think of those things it ruins my day

I wrote this poem thinking it would help
the truth is it did

I know those two lines didn't rhyme
but all the best poets don't rhyme all the time

Kristen Miller

Party Time

Went out last night
Had a blast at the party.
It felt so right
And yet so wrong.
I spoke all the words
They performed all the moves.
Amongst all the nerds
The games went so smooth.
We drank this
We drank that.
It was total bliss
Until the sun shone through.
Before sunrise
After a calm broke out.
A plan we demised
To again meet.
At dawn
We said later.
Necessary brawn was not
Goodbye is forever.

Shadlynn Burch

My name is Shadlynn. I started writing poetry when I was fourteen. Poetry is a way for me to express myself as well as tell my view of things. Usually my poetry is based on things that I have seen or personally experienced so that I can take almost any word and write about that subject. I have very few poems about other things. When I wrote this poem, I was with several friends. We were having a good time. We were laughing and joking around. My friends inspired me to write this one because of the great time.

on the edge

what do you say to someone who has already made up their mind?
when they want to die and their mind unwind?
there ain't no rhyme that could describe
the feeling of space and time
come crashing down on you, harder than you can hold
be bold,
reach out your hand,
reach to that ledge then stand,
and watch a man make a conscious decision between life and death.
you wanna know what happens next?
well i do too,
i'm tryin to help this fool.
he doesn't realize how much he means to the world,
everybody waiting, watching his curls,
waiting for a twitch to see when he fell.
i can't spell
out what i need to say,
chris james reed, we need you to stay.
hold on to this life,
go get yourself a wife,
and try to say, "i'm glad to be here and free in our great country"
and just want to be
hanging out in your backyard with me.

Tess Claycomb

My full name is Honestessie Evyenia Claycomb. I am fourteen years old and I came up with these words when talking to an old friend on Facebook. He was suicidal and at first I was just trying to help a friend, but when I found out he was okay, I finished the poem. I am very appreciative to everyone in my life, Anna Weydeveld, for always being there for me. I want to dedicate this poem to a few people. Chris James Reed, thanks for being my best friend for so long, Sam Simmons, thanks for always supporting me and helping me through tough times, Christi Claycomb, my mom, thanks for believing in me and all of your support I also want to thank Gibson, Seth, Bryant, Olee, Colby, Tanner and Casey Racki, thanks for the friendship, caring, humor, the good times and the help during the bad times.

Take This Heart

Take this heart that's left wide open
Take this heart leave words unspoken
Take this heart that hurts so much
Take this heart that doesn't mean much
Take this heart I love you so
Take this heart and help it grow
You take this heart and I'll never let go

Star Patterson

I'm a kind-of-normal, thirteen-year-old girl who's always had big dreams. Writing is one of my many passions; I am always doing it. Poetry came when I needed an outlet for all of my emotions, because I have trust issues and don't feel the need to share my personal information with many. This entry was a big stretch because I secretly lack confidence. It was a friend who encouraged me to enter a poem. Now I thank them greatly for that.

In Time

Here I am, taking up my space in time.
I am the essence of being, hidden in my own energy.
I cause movement surrounding all existence!

I am here, I am there; I am.
Though I am spent, I will always be!
I can be kept or changed, rearranged;
But I will always be the same.

I stand still, yet I run in silence.
I am invisible and cannot be touched
Yet you know I am there with you!
You feel my countenance,
and you know my urgencies.

My worth cannot be measured,
My value is most treasured.
Watch with me or without me,
Be in me or about me.
Try to stop me...I march on!

I cannot give you more than you can have of me
Because we are always together...in time!

Time!

Karita Altieri

Expressing myself poetically for my inner being since childhood has been an amazing journey. This poem was written when I was at a place in life contemplating my purpose and who I am. What might I contribute to life while I am here? Through the years, I have written poetry and filed it away. Some of it makes me laugh, some of it makes me cry. It stirs my emotions. All is from my heart of love. Though I will leave in time, I will still be here because through my writings you have known me!

You're My Entertainment

Baby you're my love,
You're as beautiful as a dove
I've never seen eyes like yours
You're as famous as Michael Kors

Baby you're my entertainment
You pick me up when I'm down
Baby don't you ever frown
Because I'll always be around
I'll always be your fan and stand by you
Because you never make me feel blue

I said you're my entertainment
You keep it live
And you've got that great vibe
I'd never miss a second with you
There ain't another thing that I'd do
Baby I love you

Victoria Cincotta

Spring Is Near

The raindrops fall upon the heads
Of flowers still curled up in bed
The time has come for them to wake
To stretch their limbs, to concentrate
And raise themselves up through the ground
Slowly upward without a sound

The big oak tree, his branches limber
Is slowly waking from his slumber
Buds are sprouting vivid green
A sight so awesome it must be seen
He is preparing for the flock
On their way timed like a clock

As I lie watching clouds go by
They seem to dance up in the sky
To rhythms of all newborn things
The time has come, let's welcome spring

Emily Webster

I am a ninth grade student at West Mount Secondary School in Hamilton, Ontario, Canada. This poem was written as part of an assignment in my ninth grade English class.

Lost

In a silent state she sits
Hoping not to cry,
And to the window turns
Her saddened emerald eye.
A tear slips out
She wipes it gone,
Blinks at the morning light.
In mourning she lies
From sunrise to sunset.
She feels the dark,
It shadows over her body,
Mind, soul and heart.
Love betrayed her
Time and again.
This time it hurt more
Than any other pain she knew.
Recover she tried
But so failed her heart,
For she could not live
That world apart.

Bethany Thomson

I'm Here

I'm here
I might be gone,
But here I stay.
There's no one else
That loves you more,
You might not see,
But here I am.
In your heart
Is where I stay.
Friends we were,
But so much more.
Lost in love,
We were blind,
We could not see
The tragic end.
Now I am gone,
But here I lie
Inside your heart.
Just you and I,
That's what we were.
Now love is gone,
Let the bugle sound.

Mica Bernhardt

The Girl

Her voice echoed off the empty walls of her heart
She stands in the full room no one looks, no one sees
The girl screams out but no one hears
She tries to get someone's attention but the darkness pulls her back
The more the darkness consumes her the more she wonders
She reaches out for help but her grip weakens
Her body slips deeper and deeper into the black hole of her heart
The ground around her caves in on her
She tries to breathe but it's too hard
The more she fights the harder it is to move
She struggles, it's useless, she fights, it's pointless
Her body broken and beaten
She waits in the dark, the cold, to be found and saved
The darkness gets darker
Her eyes close, she counts, she waits…
She wonders is she dreaming? Is she dead?
They didn't see her, they didn't hear her, they didn't feel her
Her mind races, she is scared, she is alone
The last bit of air fills her lungs
The fight is over, she lost

Kimberly Griffin

Lions

As I strum,
the furious lion rumbles.
Each note that is played
creates a different roar.
Sometimes
he roars happily,
fast,
and loud.
Sometimes
he roars sadly,
slow,
and soft.
Each rumble
has a feeling
hiding behind it.
When he roars fast,
it's like he is hunting on his prey
with one goal in mind…
To execute his melody
flawlessly.

Kaitlin O'Dowd

It Feels Good Missing Him

It feels good missing him
because he is back in my life again.
Once again, he's my one and only,
My precious jewel, my gem.

It feels good missing him...
for what was almost lost is found.
Love is in the air and it feels sweet.
A world of hope and peace abounds.

It feels good missing him.
Whatever life may bring,
I can face with power and strength...
for the coldness of the winter has turned to spring.

It feels good missing him.
The years will never take away
our chance to start anew
For God has come and rescued us and given us this day.

It feels good missing him.
It's God's and only God's majestic way
reigning down His grace on us
to give us this glorious day in May.

It feels good missing him.
So I will give thanks to the Lord above
in prayer and thought and deed and song
for this heavenly gift of love.

Rebecca Almeida

Baby Girl

Precious baby girl
Sent from above
A sweet little angel
Conceived in timeless love.

Her first curl of hair
Lacy socks and dresses
She'll even look adorable
Making sticky messes.

Wrapped around your finger
She'll know just what to do
Bat her long eyelashes
And say "Mommy, I love you!"

She'll look to you for guidance
As she grows through the years
You'll share lots of laughter
And even a few tears.

From diapers to graduation
You'll raise a lovely lady
Congratulations, Mommy
On your beautiful new baby!

Kari Costa

I'm a twenty-nine-year-old registered nurse from Pittsburgh, PA (Go Steelers!). I've been happily married to my loving husband since may 2008. Writing poetry has always felt like therapy. It's a way for me to put my emotions on paper. My mom has been writing heartfelt poetry for years. My brother and I have been fortunate enough to inherit her gift. She has been and will always be my inspiration. This poem was written as a baby shower gift for a friend of mine. The best gifts are those that come from the heart!

When I Look at You

When I look at you, do you know what I see?
I see braveness, I see hope, I see the truth.
I see someone who will always be there.
I look at you when the waves flood the shores.
When I don't know where to go, you are there.
When my world is falling down you help me pick up the pieces.
I will always look at you with respect.
You will always understand me.
You would never judge me.
I will always love you, I will never leave you.
You see what I see in the world
You help me with the pain I can't cope with.
You see what nobody else sees, you see…me.
That's what I see when I look at you.
That's how proud you make me.

TaKya Hughes

Free to Be You

Life comes in many shapes and sizes
From experience a person rises
The events that happen make you who you are
Don't keep your emotions bottled up in a jar

Strength is standing up after you fall
Courage is being willing to risk it all
Faith is knowing who you are
Risks are all part of life's game of cards

Rolling through life's unusual ocean
Friends and family show loving devotion
Ready for what life throws at me
Letting my hair down I feel free

Everyone hurts everyone feels pain
Lessons from mistakes we all learn to gain
Smiles to go, no not for me
This smile will last for eternity

Every breath that you take
Every beat your heart makes
Shows how strong you really are
Dreams and goals will take you far

Hope Davidson

A Smile

Worth more than cash
And feels uplifting
Looks so sweet
And never bitter
When one is sullen
Or feels depressed
A smile gives a bit of hope
It's like a rock
Thrown in a lake
It too provides
A ripple effect
Whoever gets
This tender gift
Is sure to pass it on to others

Michelle Spivak

And the World Cries Wicked

Two sides of the same coin, two parts of the same struggle,
each generation strains under more weight and starts to buckle
as foreign investors appraise the worth of the land,
the local farmer sheds a tear and stares at his hands,
as construction crews urge the child to drop his dead mother's arm,
the child looks up at them with fear and alarm.
And in the West, the rich justify the poor's disposition,
mock concern, oh yes, it's an alarming condition.
This is the slavery to which we've been raised,
the hypocrisy of democracy can continue for days,
America, land of the thieves,
where ideology is cheaper than bark on the trees,
America, the land of the lie,
where the children of the poor happily die,
And yet, America, the ultimate battleground for truth over lies,
It's where you stand that is the ultimate surprise.

Phillip Emanuel Hooper

*Poetry is the music that lives within the void between our intellect and soul; it is
the hymn of the human condition.*

River Way—Hot Lava—Sparkle

Green sparkle water with hot lava
The fish might die
Water rises
Green like tomorrow, green like today
This would have to be right if this were not
I would be sad
I have you, my sparkle water

Ryan Oppt

Lo, I Will Be with You

Lo, I will be with you when things are good.
I'll be with you when things are bad.
I will be with you when things are happy,
when things are sad.
I'll be with you through the rain.
I'll be with you through the pain.
I promised you.
Lo, I am with you even until the end of the world.
I'll be with you when you are up.
I'll be with you when things are down.
I'll be your endless friend
when on no one else you can depend.
I am faithful and true,
I will be with you until the end,
through the thick and thin.
This is my promise,
I am with you until the end of the world.

Delphine Price

God is awesome and faithful. I give God all the honor, glory, and praise. God is like no other. He died for me. I am so thankful for my family's, church family's, and friends' support and prayers. God's word is true. I have learned to walk by faith. I have learned to trust, believe, and obey the Christ, no matter what the situation or circumstance in my life. God is with me. He is an endless friend when no one else you can depend on. He promised me that He is with me even until the end of the world.

Childhood

Oh, how its laughter rings inside
like a bell that just screams joy.

Oh, the innocence it captures,
making every moment, every word
mean so much more.

Oh, the honesty it allows,
unparalleled in everything else.

Oh, how carefree it is,
with no thought other than the moment.

Oh, the time it has to spend,
filled with nothing but nothing
and every minute lasts so much longer.
It thinks it'll never end, and it doesn't matter,
it doesn't care because it knows it won't.
Until it does
suddenly.
And everything comes crashing down on you
because it can't hold anything up for you anymore.

You think you've wanted this
but you haven't, it has
because when this time came, it got to leave.
Abandoning you, you're lost
to fend for your own
while it slips deviously away, laughing all the way.
Slipping away from you
and falling away forever.

Sydney Lewis

I think that every poem is interpreted differently by each person that reads it based on how it makes them feel. This is one of the most beautiful things about poetry—that so many feelings can be put into the words, allowing the author to share them with the world while still creating a unique experience for each reader. When I wrote this poem, I was thinking about growing up and the changes and responsibilities that come with it. I think the protective blanket called youth hides a complicated world, but how you interpret it is completely up to you.

If I Was to Die

If I was to die at an early, young age
may everyone I know truly acknowledge my pain.
I lived my life trying to find my purpose
while walking this earth and not feeling real certain.
I made some mistakes but I learned from my past
if I'm guilty of anything it's your love I demand.
When Judgement Day comes I know I'll be blessed
because my heart is a genuine, kind mess.
If I was to die at an early, young age,
just carry my memory and the writings I gave.

Thomas L. McRae

My poetry is a gift from God and no one else. His love and presence inspires me to write and express my creative side. I'm grateful to my family and friends as well as their support and all-around love for me. I know my words have meaning and I hope they can touch many lives in a positive and constructive way.

Daybreak

Rather beast, rather brute
Willing to battle in the beauty
Of a sinuous, violent nature
He is panting as he steals his prey.
An all-consuming force
There is no middle ground.
He glides as darkness replaces dawn
All or nothing—
An elegant demon.

Alice Robinson

I have always loved poetry. It is always wonderful to be published—to be thought of as a poet worthy of being read by others. This acknowledgement is also important to the students I teach. They must submit a poem for publication. I am thrilled when they are accepted, it is a feeling that we share and cherish.

All I Ever Need

I don't have to see you
To know you love me.
I don't have to see your smile
To know you care.
All I need to is to know that you are there.

I don't need to look in your eyes
To know your heart's desires.
I only need to know
What you are thinking.

It's a feeling, love is,
That can't be seen, and although
I wish you were here with me,
Just knowing you love me
Is all I ever need.

Melissa Brown

The Red Rose

The red rose was all alone
It was gradually dying due to melancholy.
The petals were curling up as they turned pitch black with sadness.
Soon it could no longer stand up on its own.

The red rose called out to anyone for help
But nobody came.
And the people who did come just threw it on the floor
Without a care in the world about its health.

The red rose was about to die and wither away
But then a man came by it and picked it up.
The man wasn't like the others, he was filled with love.
The man took off the dead petals of sullen
And brought it back to life with his happiness.

The man then said, "I am the way and the truth and the life..."
The red rose started to rise up again and bloom.
"Come to me, all you who are weary and burdened,
and I will give you rest," the man said, as he loved it.
The red rose was now happily alive and it felt free,
No more sadness or hopeless melancholy.
Jesus Christ has saved me from my terrible ending.

Mariah Espinosa

I wrote this poem to describe my life before Christ. Depression was slowly draining the life out of me and it almost caused me to take my own life several times. I honestly felt hopeless with the rude comments from bullies, friends, and family. The loneliness I felt from being rejected and alone was overwhelming. Then, God came into the picture and I realized I am worth something. I am loved, God is my friend, God is my Father. I am a princess, a daughter of a King, Daddy's little princess. I am somebody and I have a future. God loved me and changed me.

Drop the Gun!

Ready...Aim...Fire!
Repeatedly, you pull the trigger,
You shoot me down to lift you higher,
Every shot makes the hole in my heart bigger.
Wish you could feel how great,
With every hurtful insult you throw,
Judgement hurled out of hate,
You cause the pain inside to grow.
Willingly, I admit I have sinned,
I readily recognize my mistake,
Constant conviction has got me pinned,
The repentance you see is not fake.
Yet, here I stand as the accused,
A fresh victim for you to target,
With words that only sting and bruise,
Making it impossible for me to forget.
Assuredly, my accuser is no stranger,
It is the face of someone I deeply love,
Whom I thought would love me even through danger,
And now refuses to give the love from Above.
How I wish I could turn back time,
Erase every single miserable mistake,
But it is impossible to undo the crime,
Can't you see how you are causing me to break?
In surrender, I cry out to God on my knees,
On His grace and forgiveness, I am founded,
Drop the gun and stop shooting please,
Don't you realize I am already wounded?!

Laurissa Gerritse

Perspective

Infinity on the edge of the sky
leaves me looking down
Seeking a realistic path
far below the clouds
The universe goes too far
for fragile legs to walk
And when it all comes down to it
decisions are just talk
So rest your weary legs
ease your tired mind
Things will be okay
Everything is fine

Sam Hill

Passing Dreams

Cold, endless nights,
whispers in the dark,
all my thoughts spinning around,
memories I'll never forget.
Breathing in the cold air,
looking up into the sky
while lost in my memories
and full of emotions
from the past to this very moment,
longing to know the future
as I surrender my life
to start a new beginning,
embracing myself for the bumpy roads ahead,
my mind is spinning inside.
My thoughts and emotions rushing,
rushing through my head
but settle to a stop,
as I look into the sky
at a cold endless night.

Ruth Stephenson

*I am seventeen years old and love poetry. I write my poetry about the events,
feelings, hopes, and dreams I have or have had in my life. My poem's a reflection
of my feelings in foster care. God has blessed me with a new life.*

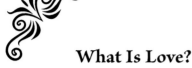

What Is Love?

Love is something everyone searches for
Desires to have in their life
But nobody really knows what love is
Or a way to really describe it
So what is love?

It's when you're only happy when you're together
When their happiness is more important than your own
When you can't get them out of your head
And all you see or think about is them

It's being there for each other day or night
Treating each other with respect
Making things work from a distance
Being able to depend on them and trust them

My heart skips a beat every time I see you
Your touch leaves a tingling trail on my skin
Hearing you say my name makes me smile
Your kisses are the most amazing ever
Being in your arms is when I'm the happiest

I look into your eyes and I can see our future
Moving in a little apartment together
Getting married and getting a house of our own
Starting a family and kids running around at our feet
Growing old together and having grandkids
Living our lives together, every day, to the fullest
You are my love and my everything

Amanda Heidemann

The Heart of the Warrior

She took me in as one of her own
She said the now is where I call home
The Dao is where my Spirit flows!
I asked her, why do you walk this road?
It's for the souls of new and old
So they can see a brighter day
I felt her presence as she walked away
her hair long and grey
countless moons that she fought and stayed
Not once did she turn away
Not once did she lose her gaze
In the morning sets her heart right
sharpens up her sword
with a stroke of light
ready for the fight
keeps death to her left side
knowin' it can touch her
take her out of the game
meditates on her aim
Many times did the walls cave
with her back against the fence
but she didn't flinch
if there's a warrior then
there's a way!

Billy Knight

This poem is the first verse of a song written in loving dedication to the life and teachings of Shaman Elder Maggie Whals. I remember the first time I got to visit and stay with Shaman Maggie. Oh, it was such a gift. Her example of living life made such a big impact on my heart. She brought so much healing and change to my reality. Every single moment and breath became a poem. I am honored to have met such a warrior. With love and gratitude, Aho.

If We'd Been Friends

I could have stayed if we'd been friends.
But you left nothing for me to hang onto.
I would have stayed if we'd been friends.
But there was nothing left of me and you.

I learned to cope and do without
the love that should have been mine.
I learned to do without your love.
If only you could have been kind.

I could have stayed if we'd been friends.
When did it all go wrong?
I would have stayed if we'd been friends.
When did we stop hearing our song?

I thought I'd cried out all of my tears.
I was sure my tears were all gone.
But here I am crying again,
Crying through the night until dawn.

No longer lovers, no longer friends,
A life filled with empty tomorrows.
Learning to care and repair myself,
Learning to let go of the sorrows.

Janet Foor

Janet Foor is a wife, mother, and grandmother. After a rewarding career with the Pennsylvania Emergency Management Agency (PEMA), she retired in 2005 and she and her husband moved to North Carolina to be near their grandchildren and watch them grow up. She enjoys attending activities for the grandchildren, her flowers, reading, and writing poetry. Poetry is a relatively new creative venture. Most of her poetry is written about nature, family dynamics, memories, and relationships.

Trees

Looking through my windowpane I've seen
A summer tree with foliage green
Or a tree of autumn as I stare
It sheds colored leaves with utmost care
Next I spy snow on the side of a winter tree
Shivering there for you and for me
Now a spring tree is easily seen
Featuring tiny pink blossoms with sprigs of green
Trees are special wherever they are
Enjoy them up close or from afar

Coralee Vernelle Haas

As I awaken each morning, I marvel at the miracles of nature so carefully planned by God. My husband Donald and I have been married for sixty-one years, and I have been blessed with nine children, thirty-one grandchildren, and fifteen great-grandchildren. We enjoy being together, weekly church services, and attending school functions in which family members participate. Writing poetry is one of my hobbies. Others are cooking, crafting, reading, sewing, and traveling, We are still living in the home we built together fifty-six years ago near Omer, the smallest city in Michigan.

The Art of Love

I fancy the sculpture the detail transcendent
Foundation striking no cause for amendment
Unforeseen its style, its flare so wild
Texture so complimenting, pure as a child
To keep in my possession am I greedy not to share?
Time in my locket everlasting I stare
Exceptional I proclaim, I am right to declare
Unwise to assume I'd stray from its lair
My only necessity like money, like gold
Is this sculpture before me, confident and bold
It is my idol, my strength, my obsession
When others observe, I cause intervention
For others to learn its true beauty, its rareness
Jealousy bleeds in the presence of their awareness
Think what you may of my love, my persistence
Understand if you can, why I worship its existence
Judge if you must, I stand proud in this trial
This passion will live on despite orders of exile
I shall not speak aloud, yet vow to be silent
The comprehension of my love shall grow to be heightened
I will die to protect it should someone get violent
In heaven I'll return by its side never frightened
No fear lies within me for you define why I'm breathing
And I'll forever be indebted to you making this life worth dreaming

Sophia Inesta

Words are magical. They have the power to possess such beauty and grace when placed together with passion. I am a writer who fell in love with someone who thought they'd never be enough. The depth of his love was as if I'd found a hidden treasure. His love was like fine art that had never been discovered or appreciated. All art needs to be loved, all art has a purpose, and all art is beautiful. Love is art is love and your art matters. Eric, you are my art and soul.

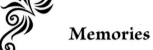

Memories

Rip my heart from out my chest
Watch me bleed upon the floor
Take the air from out my lungs
Watch as I collapse and struggle for words

All that I thought I ever knew
The memories that haunt my dreams
The sorrow, the joy, the pleasure, the pain
All these things so familiar to me

Thinking back at what I did to you
I've never felt so alone
The wounds still sting and burn
I try so hard to forget

I've felt this way for so long now
I never thought it would end this way
I'm trying hard to tell myself
That it was meant to be this way

Now you've left me here
Alone again just like the first time
You tell me you didn't mean for it to end this way
You try to tell me you still care

I try to move on with my life
Day by day I try so hard
To keep this pretend smile from fading
To keep myself from breaking down again

I hope one day I can learn to forget you
I hope the scars you left fade away
Just to feel a sense of normalcy
To not be weighed down by the memory of you

Nikoru Yoake

The Gift

Your warmth, strength and love cannot be measured in words.
You have enriched my life.
Even though there can be no light without experiencing the dark,
how beautiful a day can be when your love and kindness touch it.
You know the song in my heart and can sing it back when I have
    forgotten the words.
For you my heart has no bottom and your love leaves a memory no
    one can steal.
I will always remember what a blessing you are.
You are my gift.

Tracy A. Banks

The inspiration behind my poem is my husband Curtis Banks. He works very hard and is a very loving man. He truly is a blessing to our family. He is the music in my heart.

Swallow

Each time I cry the tears never seem as deep as a river full of fish giving
birth to new life
Each time I cry wind blows as hard as the smell of fresh cologne passing
by passengers walking down a crowded street
Each time I cry a crow turns to look at me and never blink but speaks
the language of understanding during the time of mourning calls
Each time I cry bodies of animals lie everywhere on the streets where I
drive as an sign of times to come
Each time I cry words so harsh and so powerful allow God's people to
worship and celebrate the rebirth of hatred
Each time I cry songs create the melodies that speak the language
unknown to man and can only be heard by God
Each time I cry one day will be the last day I cry no more

Rachael J. Chambers

Why?

Why is the one I love the one to treat me so terrible?
Why is the one I love the one who doesn't care about me?
Why is the one I love the one who lies about loving me?
Why is it that I had to fall for you?
Why is it that I had to fall for the lies?
Why is it that I had to fall for the false looks?
Why is it that I can't just move on?
Why me?
Why me?
Why?

Elizabeth McKee

Hate and Love

I hate you, I hate you
For what you've done to me
I hate you, I hate you
For leaving me in agony
You've left me all alone in this world
Now I have no one to hold when I am cold
But I love you
I love you so dearly
For you are in my heart so dear

Kahea Nakila

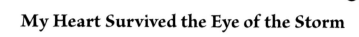

My Heart Survived the Eye of the Storm

Heartaches hit so fast
not even I knew what hit me.
Jolts of lightning striking deep within
to reshock my heartbeat.
Mother Nature's weather
clearing my mind to see her signs to warn me.

My heart survived the eye of the storm

Blackened clouds in a circular motion
above me so truly hypnotic.
Wicked wind surrounds me
creating a protective tornado around me.
Red and white roses start
floating around me trying to ease the hurt within me.

My heart survived the eye of the storm

Howling female wolves
circle me covering my cry so none can hear.
Heart of mine has deeply
hit full thrust heart aching despair.
White female wolf's spirit shoots
strength and love in me so pure so rare.

My heart survived the eye of the storm

Mother Nature's wondrous storm
opens a pathway for me to walk through.
Eagles I see flying soaring
screaming above me in the sky so blue.
Eagles wrap their wings around me
whispers I hear how can anyone ever hurt you?

My heart survived the eye of the storm

Eagles' wings brushing me over
luring me to lie down and finally rest.
Eagle downing slowly starts
covering me so firmly preciously pressed.
Mother Nature's purifying me
she always seems to know what's best.

Gloria Ashacker

I am blessed with my poetic blessings. I started writing poetry to set myself free deep inside my soul. I am a spiritual lady and my poetry tells it all. I live in Ashacker, British Columbia with my husband, George, our five daughters, Aretha, Destiny, Leanne, Farrah, Devonne and our grand-daughter Aaliyah Tate.

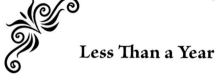

Less Than a Year

Day by day,
My life seems to fade away
From what I once thought was my new beginning,
But I find myself sinning
Over and over again.
Trust me, I'm not proud of who I've been.

I could only wish my life was filled with complete bliss,
But that single kiss
Could change my whole life,
Although it seems as if every day is a constant strife
Between me
And what could be.

My future is less than a year long,
So I must learn to be strong.
I should make the most of my time,
Before I have to make the climb—
Or rather the fall—
To meet the devil in person, who was behind it all.

Olivia Garcia

My inspiration for my writing is the beauty of life and all the little things no one takes into account anymore. I hope my poems inspire people, give them a feeling of happiness to be in this world, and have the life they have. My idea for this poem is to show that no one is perfect and we all sin, yet we're all alike in our wants and needs, so there is no reason to judge people because of their sins and the life they live.

Starving Artist

When all the pictures have been taken,
glanced at but not considered,
when all the words have been written,
half of them never read,
when the teachers give up because no one will listen
and electronics take over,

What will we do?
In a world that appreciates quantity over virtue,
starving artists just starve.

Ashleigh Shirley

Without a Dream

Insightful and colorful with mystery
Like an endless rainbow that flows over the mountains,
Our dreams swim in and out of the reflection of its waves,
Trailing through the darkness in search for the light.
Not knowing what lies ahead, we seek for the purpose of
Its gift, our new reality and fate given by the universe.
We do not see where it will take us, but we must
Trust ourselves and lead with confidence,
Undisturbed by the insecurity of guidance
And live with the belief of failure.
Even though our future is revealed in time,
We push towards our dreams through the black curtain.

Brandy Olofson

My name is Brandy Olofson, I am a freshman in high school in Paker, CO. I wrote this poem during the winter when I was up in the mountains with a few good friends. At that time, everyone around me knew what they wanted to do after they graduated from high school, and I still have no idea what I want to become. That is why I named my poem "Without a Dream." My poem describes what I feel as I continue to search for my future. I am honored to have my poem published.

I Wish I Were in Cali

I wish I were in Cali.
I wish I were free.
I wish I was with my sister there close by me.
I wish I was with Reagan to have a fun fancy free.
I wish I could be there to taste Jordan's pasta alforni.
I wish I were there in Nots Berry.
I wish I could be with Jill to laugh and be free.
I wish I could be there to see the towers, O gee.
I wish I were there to hear them laughing with me.
I wish I were in Cali, but time to wake up to reality.

Eldon Kochel

Loving You

Did you ever wonder why I love you so?
There are many reasons
some you'll never know
One of them is caring
which you always do
That one's most important
That's why I love you

Cynthia A. Leonard

Cynthia A. Leonard, age fifty-five, resides in Moultonborough, NH. She married Barry S. Leonard Sr., in 1978. They have two children, Barry Jr. and Vanessa, and two grandchildren, Parker and Trey. My husband was the inspiration for this poem. He is very caring and giving. He is not selfish, he always puts me first. We have fun going to the movies, out to dinner, walks in the rain, and playing in the snow. Barry is my everything.

Iron Chains

These iron chains that bind my feet
are cruel embodiments of my defeat.
They grasp my hands and lock my head;
I cannot bear these bonds of dread.

Heavy lays this weight of pain;
My hopes of freedom die in vain.
Faith, where have you fled?
Despair has filled my soul like lead.

Bound and beaten, here I lay,
while doubt and fear on me weigh.
And yet,
Though they burden and constrain,
I have come to love these chains.
For these chains that lash and lock and bind
cannot hold me in my mind.

And I have won against my chains;
no longer do I feel their pain.
For in being bound, I found release,
and in my chains, I found peace.

Jake Thompson

I firmly believe that the highest form of self-expression is writing. It is through my work that I strive to wholly convey my soul and mind as well as my views. I hope the world may know of the freedom that is to be gained through suffering. Thank you for reading my poem.

Your Dream

What is a dream if dreamt by another?
Or rather, who owns a dream if it is dreamt by one person, yet carried
out by another?
If a dream is a seed planted in the spiritual chamber of the heart
yet is planted by the owner of the dream rather than the owner of the
heart
who waters the seed?

I peer through eyes that long and gleam
I peer through eyes to find my dream
I peer through eyes with my brain at wonder
I peer through eyes that leave my heart asunder

For my dream I will await
and set the patience that is my bait
to find the dream that will be grand
I must put footprints in the sand

to my comrades that search night and day
lay your search along the bay
so we can find our soul's desire
and set the waves of dreams inspired

I torment myself, yet there is no need
at the door step of life, worry I bleed
I'm afraid of living the life of a fraud
so I try to put my faith in God

though at times it seems He's left me, hopeless
crossing the bridge of life, ropeless
yet I soon see I cannot fall
because among God's angels, I stand tall

And with this height I will search and seek
to find my dream and the joy it will reap
because your life is your tree
and you must water your seed

Davis Moore

I am seventeen years old. This is the best poem I've written outside of school. I've been told that I am pretty good at writing, but I haven't pursued it until now. I decided to write this poem because being on the verge of my life, this is how I feel. I just wrote what my heart felt.

The Song of the Wind

I whisper gently,
Like water on the stones,
I sigh through the trees,
Who shudder at my moans.

I'm travel worn, tired,
So many seasons have I seen,
But still when I am angered,
My bite is strong and keen.

But now as I drift,
With no storm beneath my wing,
I am gentle, soft and quiet,
So pause and hear me sing.

Charissa Beth Roberson

This poem was written as a part of a book I am writing, called The Emerald
Stone. *It is set in a magical land called Enchandya. There, all of nature has its
own unique song. Those belonging to a special group, the Emerald Light, can hear
these songs. A young girl belonging to the Emerald Light but new to Enchandya,
hears her first song while walking through the Kernian Woods as the wind rustles
through the trees. This poem is what the wind sings.*

Stay Strong

I promise I'll stay strong,
Even after a night so long.
I promise I'll be me,
Even if I think being me is hard to be.
I promise I'll smile,
Even if it takes a while.
I promise I'll try my best,
Even though I might be stressed.
You told me "When days go wrong
To always, and I mean it, always stay strong."

Laila Ramirez

Peaceful Feeling

Peaceful feeling on a mountain high
where all the snow birds have a place to lie,
wild eagles fly gracefully into the sky,
rapped water rumbling from the river close by.

In the distance my eyes fall upon the embers of a camp fire,
admits the stately trees, as though stolen like a thief in the night.
The wolves pierce at the moon, it's the lonesome call of the wild,
sitting alone feeling the cool summer breeze
and en-winded with Mother Nature I belong.

Ronalda Williams

A Son's Love for His Mother

A son's love for his mother is always true.
I know I can always count on you.
Whether I'm far away or by your side,
My love for you will not subside.
A son's love for his mother is like a precious gem,
You know I will be back to see you again.
I'd do for you whatever I can,
Even though I'm in a distant land.
A son's love for his mother is very clear,
I'll never forget you my mother my dear.
I have a strong family to pick up my slack,
Until one day when I come back.
A son's love for his mother will never lack,
A hug and a kiss and a pat on the back!

Kenneth Sandor

This poem was written and inspired by my mother, Sandra Sandor. I love you, Mom, and I will see you soon. I am thinking of you, Ken.

Masochists

Redness turns to blackness,
Life turns to ruins,
Dreams escape your mind,
Future leaves your palm.

No one understands anything,
No one will know what happened,
Putting your life on the edge,
Hurt but will never show it.

Feelings stay inside until this happens again,
Friends don't like it,
Don't care; it brings pleasure to the soul.

Nobody gets why we do it,
Only we could ever know why it happens like this.

Samantha Merritt

Sweet Bliss

She looks upon me with some hope,
I look upon death with a rope.
She hears my wailing,
I can hear death bailing.
She holds her hand out,
I look back out of doubt.
Death creeps over with no sound,
Apart from him I am not bound.
Upon sunlit skies,
I hear her cry
Her tears do stain that senseless sky.

Brandon Daniel

Remembering Love

Your beauty still surrounds me in every single way.
Kisses still surrender me like a winter cold, windy day.
Your hands still make me tremble when you slide your fingers on my
    skin.
Heartbeat increases quickly when I see you walking in.
Breath still leaves my body when the sunlight hits your eyes.
Ripple to a pond effect, my affection opens wide.
Coldness of my skin's away with the simpleness of your touch,
An epiphany of wonder to love someone so much.
Nevermore a wonder of tomorrow's weight will bring.
Wounded parts be mended by a gracious angel's sling.
Wing she wraps around me to straighten out my step,
A way to exhale softly when you feel you've lost your breath.
Many things she brings to me in the simplest kind of ways,
Like not a word between us spoken, but always knowing it's okay.
Perfect mother to the children of any she could be:
Grateful, loving, patient to our children's what I see.
Luck has never played a part to the intertwining of our souls.
Maybe what was broken has finally become a whole.
A whisper of my thankfulness, I hope you hear me say,
Thank you for your love, my dear, my angel every day.

Luke Sturdevant

Eternal Rest

We have been lost for all these years
But only to find that life brings so much tears.
I lie without a sound, my face lies restless on the ground
As my soul escapes my unholy body
And travels on its way, and it arrives just to stay
But I will not leave this way.

I awake…
In the asylum of the dead
As savage thoughts fill my head.
It's strange how in your dreams lie your darkest fears
But you, my love,
To lose you is my deepest fear.
The love we share brings a single tear.
It's my time to go.
I'll see you again sometime in Heaven where we never say goodbye.
I love you, my love, goodbye.
But there's so much to see tonight,
So why did you close your eyes?
And why can't I shut mine?
Be honest, my love, are you forever mine?

John Slone

Truth

The love you see shining in their eyes
Sparks flying when they smile at each other
Never wondering why they were together
The reason why everyone else envied
They were together through the good and bad

All of a sudden their love came to a screeching halt
The anger and jealousy barged in full force
And their perfect world came crashing down
Watching the shine and the sparks disappear
Before they knew it, their relationship was gone

Both acting like children not getting their way
Even though the love they shared was obvious
Hiding the proof of pain in their eyes
Not realizing what they had lost
Beginning to wonder why they were together

Losing the loving couple forever
Finally seeing that they did not calculate well
Never wanting to relive the love they shared
The beats in their hearts for each other were gone
Although their love was so strong.

Savannah Kopek

I was born on May 24, 1996. I am still in high school. I enjoy tae kwon do and writing practically everything. This poem was actually a poem I was assigned in creative writing. The idea came from a picture of my parents. This poem is about all my parents' troubles in their relationship. Poetry is my escape from the world and I have to thank poetry for keeping me going.

Lover

Chai tea simmers last night's dance,
the body temple and Pad Thai in the city,
discussing Vishnu and Buddha's poetic laws.
With you I take the middle way—
gaze directly into sunspots,
find the woman that is you.

In the shower I hear the music of traffic
making harp songs of your lemon-scented soap.

Bradley Paul McIlwain

The narratives in my poetry often stem from a desire to paint the natural world around me, exploring these images and their ultimate connection with memory. "Lover" began as an exercise using a Tibetan singing bowl with friends and the unique images in this poem are a result.

You Are

I watch you walk by, and I make sure I smile
You say that you're fine, but I know you're lying
There has to be some way to make them just stop
They think that it's funny but really it's not

Because you are better than they could ever hope to be
You keep on pushing through, don't let them keep you
From seeing the real you

Those bullies are stupid and they are wrong
Because you are amazing, you really are
You are so strong, I've seen it in you
They've shoved you down, you can stand back up

I know you can stand tall If only you try
Just don't give up, and one day you'll find
That you are really someone who's worth everything
You really can shine, do you hear what I'm sayin'?

Know that you have friends and that we care
If you ever need us we will be there
Because you are pretty, funny, clever, and strong
You're amazing, kindhearted, and that's not even all
Girl, you are perfect just how you are

Kirsi Devries

Drowning

The sky emptied its tears on me today
Sometimes the heavy burden is too much to bear.
I'm drowning in that lake the rest of you call self-pity
Hopelessly drifting among my cries no one ever hears or answers.
Life is like some twisted movie
Too bad we aren't the ones writing the script.
We all know the inevitable end.
Terror and disgust rise in my throat
But I choke them back down and walk on.

Jennifer Ricketts

Sun Roasted Puddle

These stains have corrupted my future years,
Of this, everything blurs into the milieu,
And insomnia drapes my mind,
Changing my default setting to "sleepless mode."

Doused in alcohol
As nutritious as poison,
Barred behind bamboo rods
Imprisoned by nature,

My unreliable years,
Unpromisingly never appear,
Like an ice cube in a dirty sun-roasted puddle,
Melted without residue.

Diana Stoll

I am a college student at Suffolk County Community College. I was inspired by a small pot hole puddle that was very hot. I was also inspired by Kurt Cobain's perspective of a stain. The tone is very grim due to my depression in high school. I don't think my future years are corrupted anymore, but when I was at that low of a point in my life, for some reason I wrote the best poetry I could have ever created. So, I'd like to have my older poems published someday.

Wine in the Dark

Only enough light to scribble,
such a lovely practice of pretense,
both the red on my lips
and the pen on my fingertips.
I've traced all these years
and wiped them away
like my empty bottle of ease.
How to show with evidence
the ruminations in flight!
What dusky rumors appear to mind.
I had a knowledge like Rilke in my poverty today,
the poet of the inner muse
begetting inner things.
That knowledge was a polished desk,
a wine cup full of four new pens,
sad music in the foreground.
I wanted things to grow from
a web without spiders,
where the flies could lie still
and come and go as they please—
a life of ease.
Another sip without dim light,
but only for a moment, a life's span,
reveals a sick old man's
coughing love within.

John Byrd

In college a professor once told us he read that one of the romantics wrote that a poet "was the best kind of man." The professor countered with the questionable lives of several poets and pronounced, "no he' of the worst type of men." I believe that poets vary. A poet is just a man or a woman who senses and feels things differently and without question, more deeply. They achieve the sublime when he or she can see outside their own pain or joy and are able to tap into it large meaning.

A Champion's Trial

The crowd's hearts ache
They hold their breath
Third set, tiebreak
To sudden death
With poise and grace
The moment she deserves
Sharapova calmly waits
For her opponent's serve
With a toss and a swing
The serve clips the tape
 A second serve a sure thing
Sharapova again calmly waits
The ball is tossed high
With kick and great speed
Tiebreak 5-5
Both players sensing the need
Time slows down
Sharapova's eyes narrow
With concentration's frown
Her forehand return like an arrow
It whizzes by her opponent
For a clean winner
Lost in the moment
He emotions only present within her
She steps to the line
And tosses the ball
Down the T will be fine
The window of error small
Ace! The crowd is on their feet
Sharapova looks upon the crowd
Upon the sea of loyal fans
The applause grows loud
Emotions overflowing, the greatest champion can but barely stand

Marcus Sass

Tools

God doesn't give us hearts
to watch them wither away,
He gives us tools to guide us
each and every day.
God doesn't give us minds
not to use for His glory.
Each person that touches our lives
tells his own little story.
God don't give us feelings
to make our hearts to turn them to stone,
God made Adam and Eve
so they would never be alone.
God does give us our past
so we can learn from our mistakes,
and He can heal and mend
our many heartbreaks.

Dawn Ziegler Schnapp

Two Lives

Living two lives
Which one to believe?
Trying so hard to remember the truth
Wondering
Thinking
Asking
What to do?
Which one to believe?
The second life taking over who I am
What I want to be
Hurting me
Taking my pride
Just take me away
God, just take away the pain and frustration
My mind says leave life
But my heart says no
I chose to follow my heart
And not my second life

Amneh Qutifan

Night Flowers

Tonight the stars are crystals
That gleam in darkness on high,
And as your arms hold me safe,
I hear myself whisper, "Goodbye."

Tonight the stars are falling,
And my heart's on my sleeve,
As I feel a tear run down my cheek,
And I can only watch you leave.

Tonight the stars are singing
A melancholy tune,
As everything gets darker,
And night's flowers start to bloom.

Julia McCarthy

Awaken Sinking Ship

I will show myself holy to those who come near me and before all the
people I will be glorified. (Right in front of you I see my life)
It's these cold December days that get me thinking who I am today!
I stayed quiet for way too long. You were holy and I was not.
Not worthy! Who am I without you and who are you without me?
I'll break this meaningful promise in order to be with you.
I was so afraid of the vital outcome, I chose rain over the sun.
I will show myself holy to those who come near me and before all the
people I will be glorified. (Right in front of you I see my life)

Antoine Airoldi

Tea

Dusk approaches as I sit alone and think,
I write these words of sorrow in a dark and nasty ink.
The candlelight flickers casting shadows on the ground.
This run-down kiln creaks with that oh familiar sound.
I may be lost in thoughts again,
And it could be all that I am.
I may be feeling regret and pain
That this nasty ink will forever stain.
But at least I'm still alright,
Another cup of tea? And then I'll say goodnight…

Katty Holburn

I could detach your mind from your body. I could take you away for just a moment and you could feel my hurt, pain, and love. I could push you deep inside yourself revealing to you your own hurt and pain, your own love. Words are powerful, but it's the combination and presentation where they gain meaning to their power. Poetry is therapeutic; it brings life to my emotions and calmness to my soul. It's an art, it's a lifestyle, and it's who I am. Poetry is a part of me, just as I am a part of poetry.

This Game

So many different choices,
they all keep me in this game.
I sometimes feel all alone,
my truth is just a shame.
My heart is with a special man,
My life belongs to him.
In this game of life I find I only want to win!

Tammy Headley

Haunted

Let me go.
Release my mind,
Freedom from your cold grip.
Escape has never been an option.
It is an impossible struggle
To sit in your shadow pleading.
You never hear my words.
Don't test my strength
For you will fail.

I no longer wish your presence
Or the pain you cause.
A plague you are,
Bringing death.

I will not be among them,
Those who end all madness.

Ignored I remain.
Mercy is not an option
To be bestowed upon you,
For you have destroyed
All innocence I had.

No longer will the guilt plague me.
The pain of my actions
You have thrived on,
And I have lost.
There is no faith.
I have no beliefs.
What have I survived?

I may live,
Yet my soul is lost.
But you don't understand,
And ruin any hope,
My dreams forever lost.

Gelene M. Beverly

Find Me

Playing on the seesaw without another on the end,
Yearning for someone to tuck me in at night,
Wanting someone to help me figure out why 3 times 4 equals 12.
Sitting at the lunch table without a single soul,
Longing to have someone to share a milkshake with,
Craving to be in that crowd,
Crying in my room because he wasn't the one,
When my parents just don't seem to get it,
When I lose a parent or a relative,
During the times where I feel like no one understands me,
After I have made those stupid teenage mistakes,
When I am just being a teenager,
As a student studying hard for that next test,
Playing my guitar as I search for my chance,
After several failed attempts to find that one person,
As I try to make ends meet,
While I am trying to find a job,
When that night out becomes a disaster,
When it seems that I just can't catch a break.
Once that marriage starts to fall apart,
When the kids start to get out of control,
At the time when I am trying to climb that promotional ladder,
While the bills are coming in but not going out as quickly,
When it seems that I just can't win for losing.
When I am alone in a hospital bed,
When I have fallen and can't get up,
Once my family has placed me in a nursing home,
Waiting on a visit,
I just want to be found.

Chelsey Guy

I have been writing since my mother passed away when I was thirteen years old, about four years ago. Since then I have been using my experiences and emotions to write stories and poems. Poetry gives me a break from the harsh and unforgiving reality of the world. It allows me to vent and to find happiness. My friend found me crying in a corner and that inspired me. I want my poetry to inspire and encourage people to dream and to love.

Brother

Glowing emeralds hold love so bright,
spheres of curiosity and sight.
Your profile eclipses the natural light,
and lays a strong shadow over the night.

As your soft kiss lands on my skin,
the moon's rays cast one again.
But before my being leaves for rest,
your message reaches my beating chest.

Taking another breath, I turn.
Silently speaking, your love I return.
As you intently watch the moon,
I know that I will dream soon.

We seldom speak, you and I.
But our love still belittles the sky.
As the night comes to an end,
there is one last message I'll send.

I never knew much of love before,
I barely believed in the existence of more.
To this day, my belief has grown,
from my first sight of the emeralds you own.

Alexandra Marika Kussurelis

The Path

Hell has given me its warmth
And brought me to the light,
The light of knowledge,
Not that of ignorance.
My mind has since wandered,
With no signs of coming back.
Even the Spirit cannot save me.
For I am doomed to seek more.
Without a guide to lead me,
I've fallen with the sinners
To a land I think I've known,
But I cannot grasp its name.
Now the cold is all around me,
Along with screams of terror.
I cannot block the sound,
For my scream is surely the loudest.
I've fallen too far down,
I cannot reach the surface.
Though I hear salvation calling,
It's not my name that's being said.
My time will come someday,
Till then I shall sleep within the fire.

Madeline McNeal

What's Inside Me

I didn't care about love or if I would hurt you through my actions.
But what I didn't know was I'd end up falling for you.
A month had passed and I wanted to talk to you more,
wanted to be with you and be held by you.
Then one day I thought I could never be the right one for you.
So I left...I didn't know how much it would bother me
leaving you, but it did. I needed you because I loved you.
It was only a matter of time before you gave me a chance.
That's when I made a promise to myself I would never leave or
ruin my second chance. Everything was perfect with me and you.
I look back to all the memories the times we've been together.
I don't know if I can live without you.
I waited this long for someone like you to come around,
Someone who gets worried when you haven't called or when
they really love you. So many people have tried to break
the lock to my heart. You may not be my best friend but
you are the one person I can tell how I really feel! I love you!

Jessica Shaw

Cemetery Aubade

Listening to the crunch of leaves
In a world so ashen and sere
I walk in the past with fear
I gaze into the future
a mirror with no reflection

The mistakes of my life have been made before
My life is a common tale
told truthfully to the world
Its days are roses left to die
and the memories that will return

These two young lovers are asleep
under the grass
They will not mind if I pass them by
much later when they are covered in snow
The love that they gave
has no power over the grave

I left the town with its smiling faces
and sleeping children
I traveled to the country
and saw the worn-out faces
and no children

I lived near the cemetery
and courted the sexton's son
Here when we were old
he buried me with his own hands
and now he sleeps at my side

Time will not let us speak
It passes by above
I am a voice from the past
dreaming of a lifetime ago above

Shanna Alpers

In My Father's Eyes

As I look into the eyes of a man
I knew to be my father,
I see nothing—
No honor,
No strength,
No Compassion.
I see nothing but a black hole
Created by nothing but lies,
Broken promises and everlasting mistakes.
But I look, I realize that
Just because a man is given the title of a father doesn't make him one.

Alexandra Weir

Change

...so if you were to ask,
What I am from yesterday?
I guess that I would say
That I never really changed.
But in a different way,
I'm not really the same.
For yesterday is yesterday,
And I've gone a different way.
So if you were to ask
And redirect the blame,
I want you to remember just what was the tame.
For what was for forever very quickly changed.
And in this newfound way,
With new words I might lay.
So you remember the past and just what was the game
And recollect the future for desires have it may.
From then on when you spoke those words, we never were the same.
And if that's what you count as change,
Then forever it's within range.
Yes—if that's what you would ask—that's what I would say.

Paityn Donaldson

Poetry means a lot to me. There is not very much inspiration behind this poem, I just liked to write. I think everyone should see life in a poetical way and to find humor in it.

Miley, My Love

Whose gift this is you cannot discern,
My heart, however, is in your possession.
I don't request anything in return,
Except for you to hear my confession.

Though I rarely display emotion
And hide my thoughts and feelings in secrecy,
Love is not something I have given much devotion,
Nor do I believe heavily in prophecy.

However, despite my pessimistic expression,
I do think love has an appealing design.
Therefore, permit me to ask you this one question, Miley:
Would you allow me to hold your heart if I let you hold mine?

Patrick McLaw

Patrick McLaw is the publisher and superintendent of Northern Imperial Publishing—his own, independent publishing company. Recently, McLaw published his debut novel The Insurrectionist, *under the name Dr. K. S. Voitaer, and will soon release the sequel,* Lilith's Heir. *McLaw currently resides in the United States of America but he intends to relocate to London, England in the distant future. As an educator, McLaw's motivation and inspiration for success comes from his mother, Kay White, and his father, Dr. David C. Ring Jr.—both of whom are dedicated educational professionals.*

Solitude

My wings droop while my feathers fall
I was an angel who had it all
But now I feel violated
And often sedated
My legs crossed and my eyes closed
I should have thought about it I suppose
I have lost my most precious possession
I gave in to someone's obsession
Tears running down my chin
Regretting the fact that I gave in
"I should have waited," I said
before lying on his bed
or waited until I got married
Worried if it could be a child I carried
My innocence is lost
But now I have to suffer the cost
Sitting on the floor crying
I can't believe I listened to his lying
But now he treats me mean and rude
That's why I sit in solitude

Shontell L. Mason

I have been through many trails and tribulations only to still come out in the end with my head held high and a smile on my face. Life is a lesson...you learn from it. Mistakes will be made but do not regret them...learn from them and use your knowledge to progress throughout your journey of life. Love it, live it and thank God. God bless.

Index

CPSIA information can be obtained at www.ICGtesting.com
Printed in the USA
BVOW060649250512

291058BV00002B/1/P